Architectural Design

The Challenge of Suburbia

Guest-edited by Ilka + Andreas Ruby

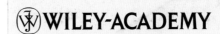 WILEY-ACADEMY

Architectural Design
Vol 74 No 4 July/August 2004

ISBN 047086687X
Profile No 170

Editorial Offices
International House
Ealing Broadway Centre
London W5 5DB
T: +44 (0)20 8326 3800
F: +44 (0)20 8326 3801
E: architecturaldesign@wiley.co.uk

Editor
Helen Castle
Production
Mariangela Palazzi-Williams
Art Director/Designer
Christian Küsters (CHK Design)
Design Assistant
Hannah Dumphy (CHK Design)
Project Coordinator
and Picture Editor
Caroline Ellerby

Advertisement Sales
01243 843272

Editorial Board
Denise Bratton, Adriaan Beukers,
André Chaszar, Peter Cook,
Max Fordham, Massimiliano
Fuksas, Edwin Heathcote,
Anthony Hunt, Charles Jencks,
Jan Kaplicky, Robert Maxwell,
Jayne Merkel, Monica Pidgeon,
Antoine Predock, Leon van Schaik

Contributing Editors
André Chaszar
Craig Kellogg
Jeremy Melvin
Jayne Merkel

Abbreviated positions:
b=bottom, c=centre, l=left, r=right

Cover photo courtesy of Lyons Architects,
Melbourne.
AD
p 4 © FAT photos Tomas Klassnik; pp 5-7 ©
Bernd Kniess; pp 8-11, 12(b), 13(b) & 14-17
© Ines Schaber; pp 12(t) & 13(t) © Jörg
Stollmann; pp 18-27 © Tanya Reith; p 28 ©
Eyal Weizman; p 29 © Daniel Bauer;
pp 30-5 & 36-7(t) © Milutin Labudovic,
images courtesy of Peace Now;
p 36(b) © BT'Selem & Eyal Weizman;
pp 38-9 © Servicio Aerofotográfico Nacional;
p 40 © Walter Schwenninger;
pp 41, 42(c&b), 43 & 44(b) © Kathrin Golda-
Pongratz; pp 42(t) & 44(t) Courtesy of Luís
Dórich Torres; p 45 © IMP, Lima;
pp 48-53 © Bernd Kniess;
pp 54-9 © Wesley Jones, J,P:A; pp 60-5 ©
Juan Pablo Molestina; pp 66-71 © cet-0/
Kunst+Herbert; pp 74-5 © 51N4E;
pp 76, 78 & 79(r) © Hélène Binet;
p 77(t) & 79(l) © Roland Halbe;
p 77(b) © Zaha Hadid Architects,
photo Roger Rothan/Airdasol; pp 80-1 ©
Lyons Architects, photos Trevor Mein;
pp 84-5 © EM2N Architekten; pp 86-91 ©
Metrogramma; pp 92, 93(tr) & 94-6
© Sadar Vuga Arhitekti; p 93(tl) © Sadar
Vuga Arhitekti, photo GZS; p 93(br) © Sadar
Vuga Arhitekti, photo Joze Suhadolnik.

AD+
pp 98 & 101 © Edmund Simmons/View;
pp 99-100 © Arts Team @ RHWL; p 102
© Markus Dochantschi, photo Eric
Schuldenfrei; p 103(tr) © Markus
Dochantschi, photo Snaap; p 103(tl & bl)
© Roger Davies; p 103(br) © Kitchen Aid;
p 104(t) © Boffi SpA; p 104(b) © Sub-Zero
Freezer Company, Inc; pp 105-8 © Philippe
Ruault; p 109(t) & 112(b) © Timothy Soar;
pp 109(b), 110, 112(t) © Gollifer Langston
Architects; p 111 © James Brittain; p 113
© Morley Von Sternberg; p 114 © Benedict
Luxmoore; p 115 © James Morris; pp 117-
21 © NOX; pp 122-4 © Tim Griffith.

Acknowledgement
We would like to thank the Architecture
Department of the University of Applied
Arts, Düsseldorf, Germany, for supporting
the research for this project. A substantial
part of the material published in this issue
originated from an online workshop made
possible by the university. In particular,
we would like to express our gratitude to
Professor Pablo Molestina who coordinated
the workshop and without whom this
project would not have been possible.

Subscription Offices UK
John Wiley & Sons Ltd.
Journals Administration Department
1 Oldlands Way, Bognor Regis
West Sussex, PO22 9SA
T: +44 (0)1243 843272
F: +44 (0)1243 843232
E: cs-journals@wiley.co.uk

Annual Subscription Rates 2004
Institutional Rate: UK £175
Personal Rate: UK £99
Student Rate: UK £70
Institutional Rate: US $270
Personal Rate: US $155
Student Rate: US $110
AD is published bi-monthly.
Prices are for six issues and include
postage and handling charges.
Periodicals postage paid at Jamaica,
NY 11431. Air freight and mailing
in the USA by Publications
Expediting Services Inc, 200 Meacham
Avenue, Elmont, NY 11003

Single Issues UK: £22.50
Single Issues outside UK: US $45.00
Details of postage and packing charges
available on request

Postmaster
Send address changes to *AD* Publications
Expediting Services, 200 Meacham Avenue,
Elmont, NY 11003

Printed in Italy. All prices are subject to
change without notice. [ISSN: 0003-8504]

08
18
48
60
74
80
84
98+
102+
105+
109+
117+

The Challenge of Suburbia

Guest-edited by Ilka + Andreas Ruby

In the popular imagination, life in suburbia is deemed to be a lesser existence. *Collins Dictionary* defines the underlying definition of 'suburban' as: 'mildly derogatory. narrow or unadventurous in outlook'. Whether a British semi or a North American subdivision, the suburban house, as the primary unit of suburbia, has come to represent all of the confines and insularity of the suburban condition, where the only movement from the dormitory settlement is the back and forth of the daily grind – the commute into the city.

The perceived banality and constrictions of suburban life have made suburbia fertile territory for film directors and novelists alike (one only has to think of the white picket fences of *The Graduate* or, more recently, *American Beauty*, which self-consciously allude to a whole Hollywood genre). The creators of these narratives are inevitably those who got away, lifting the lid on the querky or subversive undercurrents of their previous lives. Like their fellow creatives, many architects summon from the suburbs. Despite, and perhaps because of this, architecture and architectural culture remain fixated on the city, the apex of architectural achievement being the commission for the great civic, urban building – most conspicuously, in recent years, the public art gallery or museum.

Suburbia has remained strictly off limits. There is an element of snobbishness involved: Libeskind was scoffed at for even venturing to design a shopping mall. More importantly, though, the economic and planning conditions in suburbia have also tended, with some exceptions, to exclude the services of architects and made the suburbs the preserve of volume house-builders and speculative developers. It is only in recent years, in the UK at least, that the continued rolling-out of national house-types has become truly unsustainable as further limits have been placed on greenfield sites. Suburbia has been pushed back on itself. In the outer sub-urban ring of towns and cities, the need for higher densities and creative solutions has helped usher in a new era, opening up fresh potential for architectural design.

Can architects rise to the challenge of suburbia? In this issue, Ilka and Andreas Ruby are very clear about who they are talking to and with, making architectural practice the driver, rather than the receptor, of their enquiries. By featuring bold, curious, ingenious and enterprising research projects and designs by architects, they are proposing a new role for architecture in the suburbs, one that focuses on performance of building and the potentially transformative role of new structures. In full, they are throwing down the gauntlet for the architectural profession. ⌀

Right
For their installation in Selfridges' window, FAT chose to present a vision for London in which the urban is superceded by the suburban. Hoxton, Nottinghill, Islington and Camden are engraved on tombstones in the foreground. A representation of Feltham, a typical London suburb located near Heathrow airport, takes centre stage on a snooker table. *Greetings From London*, an exhibition of 10 architects' work in London Selfridges' windows was organised by The Architecture Foundation with Selfridges in June 2004.

Opposite and following spread
Suburban houses near Cologne, Germany.

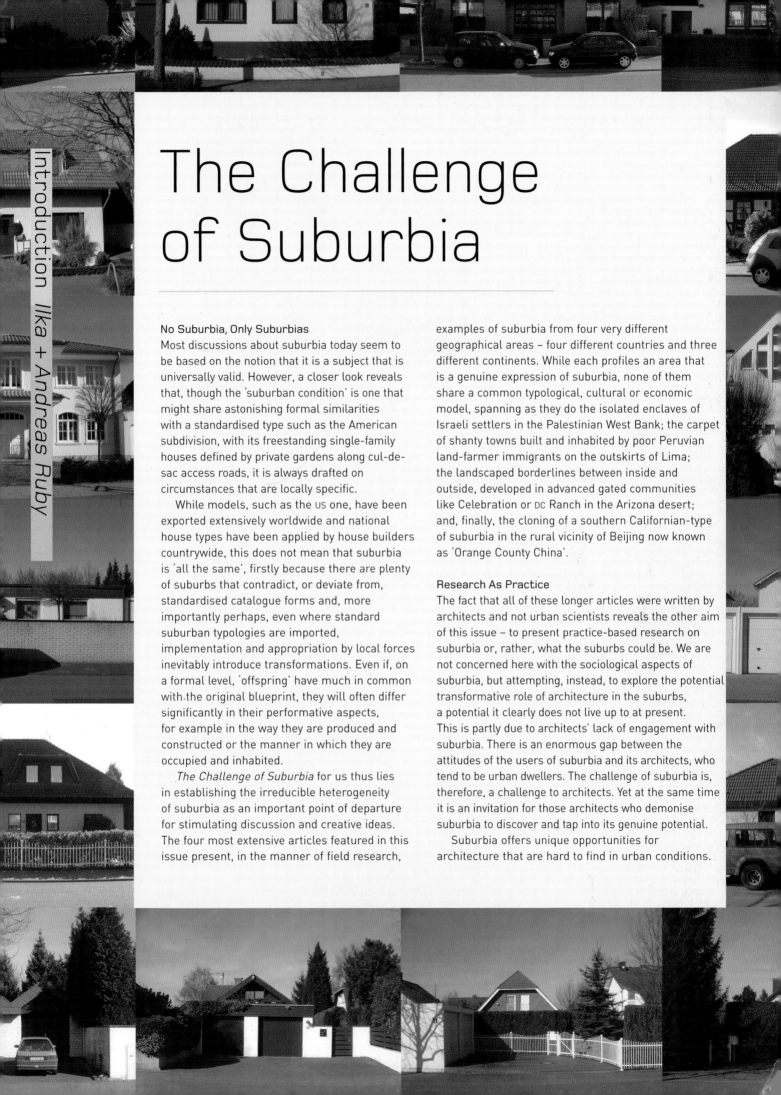

The Challenge
of Suburbia

No Suburbia, Only Suburbias

Most discussions about suburbia today seem to be based on the notion that it is a subject that is universally valid. However, a closer look reveals that, though the 'suburban condition' is one that might share astonishing formal similarities with a standardised type such as the American subdivision, with its freestanding single-family houses defined by private gardens along cul-de-sac access roads, it is always drafted on circumstances that are locally specific.

While models, such as the US one, have been exported extensively worldwide and national house types have been applied by house builders countrywide, this does not mean that suburbia is 'all the same', firstly because there are plenty of suburbs that contradict, or deviate from, standardised catalogue forms and, more importantly perhaps, even where standard suburban typologies are imported, implementation and appropriation by local forces inevitably introduce transformations. Even if, on a formal level, 'offspring' have much in common with the original blueprint, they will often differ significantly in their performative aspects, for example in the way they are produced and constructed or the manner in which they are occupied and inhabited.

The Challenge of Suburbia for us thus lies in establishing the irreducible heterogeneity of suburbia as an important point of departure for stimulating discussion and creative ideas. The four most extensive articles featured in this issue present, in the manner of field research, examples of suburbia from four very different geographical areas – four different countries and three different continents. While each profiles an area that is a genuine expression of suburbia, none of them share a common typological, cultural or economic model, spanning as they do the isolated enclaves of Israeli settlers in the Palestinian West Bank; the carpet of shanty towns built and inhabited by poor Peruvian land-farmer immigrants on the outskirts of Lima; the landscaped borderlines between inside and outside, developed in advanced gated communities like Celebration or DC Ranch in the Arizona desert; and, finally, the cloning of a southern Californian-type of suburbia in the rural vicinity of Beijing now known as 'Orange County China'.

Research As Practice

The fact that all of these longer articles were written by architects and not urban scientists reveals the other aim of this issue – to present practice-based research on suburbia or, rather, what the suburbs could be. We are not concerned here with the sociological aspects of suburbia, but attempting, instead, to explore the potential transformative role of architecture in the suburbs, a potential it clearly does not live up to at present. This is partly due to architects' lack of engagement with suburbia. There is an enormous gap between the attitudes of the users of suburbia and its architects, who tend to be urban dwellers. The challenge of suburbia is, therefore, a challenge to architects. Yet at the same time it is an invitation for those architects who demonise suburbia to discover and tap into its genuine potential.

Suburbia offers unique opportunities for architecture that are hard to find in urban conditions.

Due to their relatively short history there is less pressure on new interventions to comply with the piled-up fabric of the past.

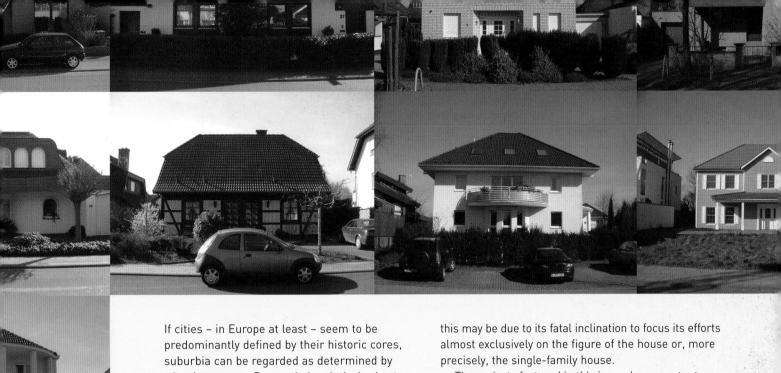

If cities – in Europe at least – seem to be predominantly defined by their historic cores, suburbia can be regarded as determined by what is to come. Due to their relatively short history there is less pressure on new interventions to comply with the piled-up fabric of the past. In fact, since its inception suburbia has been afforded a blank screen for projecting people's hopes and desires: it is the promise of a new beginning that lures city dwellers away from town centres and the negative side-effects of industrialisation and city-living, such as pollution and urban congestion. This ecology of projection has forever been at work in suburbia, no matter how absurd the results. Yet if architecture would accept this psychological predisposition it could be used as a strategic hinge to get a grip on suburbia and possibly impact on its paradigm.

The Potential of Unbuilt Space
Exploring this ecology of projection is a central concern of the architectural projects assembled in this issue. Common to all of them is the pioneering spirit that characterised the quasi-utopian mind-set of suburbia. All project scenarios onto the situation in order to encourage lifestyles (in the broadest sense of the word) that are partly informed by existing living patterns. A constitutive element common to all of them is the conscious decision to use the unbuilt, rather than the built, fabric as the main tool of intervention. In fact, if architecture generally fails to implement itself in suburbia,

this may be due to its fatal inclination to focus its efforts almost exclusively on the figure of the house or, more precisely, the single-family house.

The projects featured in this issue, however, try to move the focus of the intervention to the ground: the unbuilt space between and around the houses. In suburbia this space is most often treated as a mere infrastructural facility, its sole purpose to give access to the private realm of the houses, which gets all the attention of the private dweller. But the projects here take a complementary stance: they try to turn the (volumetrically speaking) negative space of the street into a (programmatically speaking) positive space of suburban life. Hence established boundaries between public and private are renegotiated as previously underused spaces are proposed for collective use, and public space, previously the blind spot of suburbia, becomes the site of its most relevant future development.

The longing for identity, so over-present in countless built manifestations in the private realm of suburbia, is redirected and granted gratification in the public realm, discovering, again, a new world, but with the difference that this world has been there all the time, albeit apparently unnoticed. Much like Jourdain, in Molière's play *The Bourgeois Gentleman*, who, on being asked by his philosophy master whether he wished to write a love letter to the lady of his choice in verse or prose, learns with excitement that prose is the name applied to the way he speaks, so that 'for the past forty years I have been speaking in prose without knowing it!', there is a chance that suburbia will eventually discover that it has been surrounded by public space all the time – also without knowing it. ∆

Perimeter Wondering

Experiencing the boundaries of Celebration and DC Ranch, two popular American housing developments, artist **Ines Schaber** and architect **Jörg Stollmann** analysed how landscape is used to create identity and exclusive public space in suburbia.

Right
We are on Osceola Polk Line Road, looking north. A small wire fence is separating us from the Reedy Creek Swamp, a natural preserve. Far in the distance we assume Celebration's city limits, but there is no view of the city from here at all.

'If urban culture is a complex and fluid system of borders between private and public that are often institutionalized by architectural forms, these borders, and the discipline of architecture that assist in their assertion, is never innocent.'
— Mark Wigley [1]

In his article 'Bloodstained architecture', Mark Wigley states that, opposed to a common prejudice, the essence of public space lies in its exclusive nature. First of all, public spaces have always excluded what was considered private. Second, public spaces have always been spaces to include eligible citizens and exclude others in more or less oppressive ways. Thus, the easiest way to qualify public spaces would be to identify exactly what, or whom, they exclude.

The exclusive borders and limits of public space can be read as inscriptions of what is considered the eligible public, and what is not. Following these peripheral traces, this essay describes the demarcations of two popular housing developments in the US – Celebration and DC Ranch – both of which can be considered contemporary suburban model cases for the exclusivity of public space in today's suburbia.

In order to understand the spatial and social impacts of these models on the suburban landscape, we need to look at how they not only aim to create an identity inside their confines but also how they define their relation to the outside – to what is excluded. Both communities are initiated and marketed by developers who to a great extent integrate the expertise of architects and landscape architects in the conception and realisation of their projects.

Celebration is a product of Disney Corporation, Inc. It is situated southwest of Orlando, a mile southeast of Disney World Florida. It is a non-gated master-planned community, orienting its urban layout and architecture by the ideas of New Urbanism. Thus, it is modelled after the ideal image of the 19th-century American Small Town that never existed. DC Ranch, in Scottsdale, is a development consisting of several smaller gated communities, situated northeast of the Phoenix metro area. It is one of the first master-planned 'desert communities' employing native vegetation and adobe-style architecture. The reinvented history of the place, a formerly existing ranch at the western foothills of the McDowell mountains, was chosen as the community's overall design theme. DC Ranch is built and marketed by regional developers, specified in the upscale housing market.

Both projects provide home owners with a series of services including schools, shopping, a market street, nearby health-care facilities and communal leisure spaces. Given the ambition of both developments to create an autonomous interiority, it became a crucial question for us how they define their relation to the adjacent areas and how the inhabitants and visitors perceive the location and expansion of these islands.

Celebration
The main road leading to Celebration is Route 192, connecting Disney World with the city of Orlando. Route 192 is a dense, ordinary strip with shops, restaurants, bars and hotels. At one point, a well-maintained green pasture and a white wooden fence interrupt the strip architecture. The ideal landscape of the American Small Town welcomes the home owner, and a huge billboard invites the public to enter.

The visitor is guided into the town's centre, and asked to park his or her car and proceed on foot.

Passing the village's central lake, the visitor walks along Main Street, guided by the public buildings along small shops and cosy restaurants. The private housing further away from this central street is not integrated into the line of attractions and, thus, unseen by most visitors. Beyond these residential areas, vast lands inaccessible even to its inhabitants surround the growing city of Celebration. This territory, still part of Celebration's property limits, merges with the surrounding, hardly accessible and preserved swamp areas. Thus, the town of Celebration occupies only a very small portion of the territory it claims. It is impossible to drive, or even walk, from the centre to the town limits other than on the road leading towards the two exits.

In search of Celebration's limits, we drove along the streets adjacent to its territory. From Interstate 4 we found Celebration beautifully staged, but no way to stop and leave the car. The view is constructed for the driving passers-by. Cruising on the strip, we passed Celebration the closest. But with the exception of the welcoming area, the view towards Celebration is blocked. At some point we had to drive onto a supermarket yard and climb onto our car to finally peep over a wall to catch a glimpse of a moat and Celebration's white homes beyond. Always finding ourselves kept at a distance from the town's delineations, we finally took a byroad and arrived at a vast no-man's-land without streets or pathways. Looking over the swamp that surrounds the town on three sides, we could see Celebration no more.

The centre of Celebration is busy. The visiting public and inhabitants alike are enjoying Main Street and its amenities. The Disney Corporation attracts visitors on their way to the amusement park, promising a special kind of history reinvented for today. Exactly through this public, semi-tourist character, all attention is focused on the centre and its architecture. Except for the two public entrances, the town is inaccessible from outside. Being in Celebration, the borders and areas beyond are imperceivable. The lands enabling the city to keep its distance from its adjacent, and not always trustworthy, neighbours are well integrated into the overall layout of the development, but have been altered by only a minimum of design interventions as they are not considered part of the overall visual being created.

DC Ranch

With DC Ranch, the method of approaching and picturing we had used for Celebration didn't work. Reaching its perimeter from the outside proved impossible. Its borders are situated either far up in the McDowell mountains or blocked by adjacent private developments. There is no road to drive or path to walk around DC Ranch. The only road that accesses its territory is Thompson Peak Parkway. Here, the actual gates and fences of the individual gated communities inside DC Ranch start to appear long after one has crossed the development's property line. However, as we left Pima Road to enter Thompson Peak Parkway, an increasing density of well-fed and strictly maintained desert plants was building a subtle contrast to the desert landscape outside – an enriched desert landscaping that lets a stranger know he or she is trespassing on private ground. To the home owners, it signals that they are coming home.

As it was impossible to approach the borders from outside, we had no option but to try to reach them from the inside. Leaving the parkway, we wandered in between the gated communities, searching for the development's perimeter. All of the areas we identified

4

5

Right and opposite, top
Maps of Celebration and DC Ranch with indications of where the photographs were shot.

Below
We are driving on Central Florida Greenway crossing Bronson Memorial Highway. Leaning out of our car we are able to peep over a wall. We catch a glimpse of a moat and Celebration's white homes behind. Presumably, this is not for the benefit of tourists but a deterrent against strangers who try to creep in.

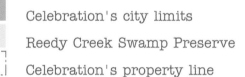

Celebration's city limits

Reedy Creek Swamp Preserve

Celebration's property line

1 mile

Below left
We are standing inside one of the gated communities of DC Ranch, looking south. A pedestrian trail and a small lawn are integrated into the landscaped desert vegetation. The landscaping zone in the foreground is designed to emulate a natural desert character. The city of Phoenix appears in the distance.

Below right
At DC Ranch's perimeter we are looking east to the mountains that are a part of the community's property. In the foreground enhanced desert planting distinguishes the street loop. In the background the landscaping slowly blends from a transitional zone behind the street to a more natural zone towards the foothills. The golf course's green lawn is inserted in between the natural desert landscaping and the untouched native vegetation towards the hilltops.

DC Ranch city limits

Mc Dowell Sonoran Preserve

DC Ranch property line

 1 mile

on the map as the limits of the territory were not recognisable as such. A subtle landscape design blended carefully from zones of enhanced desert planting to the natural desert. Border demarcations were disguised and hardly visible. The vista of the surrounding landscape was so extensive that it gave the impression of the community's interior being endlessly extended into the native desert.

We were reminded of the principle of the borrowed view. Having originated in English garden design during the 18th century, it is that of a vista extended beyond the actual property line – a design strategy that gives substance to the spectator's eye by denying the visibility of any differentiating or dividing lines upon the ground. At DC Ranch, the borrowed view not only represents a blending of private and public surfaces within the community to create the communal spaces, but also disguises the borders and edges of the property. Anything visible is considered to be the community's common ground, and serves to negate the boundaries to the outside and the possibly non-identical beyond.

A huge part of DC Ranch incorporates additional natural preserves to create a subtle transition between the areas surrounding the private plots and the edges of the development. The design propagates the impression of unlimited extension. An interior identity is created not through difference and aesthetic contrast but through a design of supposedly total visibility, expanding from inside to outside.

Islands in the Sun

Like Celebration, DC Ranch is a master-planned, strictly regulated suburban development to house several thousand future inhabitants. Both are generating an ambience aimed at defining each community's specific identity. Both tend to physically and spatially exclude the unwanted and the non-identical. But both also tell a different story. Celebration, in the tradition of the Ideal City, erases or neglects the existing place in order to build the American Small Town from scratch. The lands surrounding it are necessary, but not designed as part of the community's aesthetic. All attention is focused on the interior definition of space through the placement of architectural objects. DC Ranch also empties out most of its territory, but only to bring back the desert and its vegetation in an even more persuasive manner. The story told is one of an improvement of nature rather than subordination. Through the subtle, blending landscape design, integrating the native desert, the community propagates the exterior as a continuation of its interior space. The outside, the nonidentical, has disappeared.

In the US, suburban spaces of public gathering unmistakably serve specific user groups and exclude others. The shopping mall and the country club are exclusive places, for they control who can enter and linger and who cannot. In recent years these spaces have turned into a popular commodity on the housing market. People buying a home are looking for communal spaces specifically catered to them. They demand amenities, services and a specific character of the community with which to identify. Thus, developments include these public communal spaces within their confines and are turning into what developers like to call 'communities'. These communities could well be considered built model cases for future living. Their developers try to be so close to the market requirements that they seem to know best how people really want to live their lives. And a bird's-eye view over suburbia reveals a

multiplicity of developments transforming it into a system of clearly defined islands, each community an interior space.

Different strategies have been developed to create a homogeneous interior aesthetic and social structures: precise design guidelines for the builders and codes for the inhabitants – the so-called Codes, Covenants and Restrictions (CCS&RS). By means of legal redress, these inscribe very clear ideas into the plans of individual communities. Passing by the communities, their island character is less discernible but, on entering, the visual impression of coherence and sameness expresses the effectiveness of these legal codes. The overall aesthetic themes of the developments control and preserve the community's visual identity, that which future home-owners buy into. Here, the aesthetic of sameness functions as a social normative. Walking around the finished and lived-in communities, it is hard to imagine how to imagine what is going on in these spaces any better than the pre-completion advertising and renderings portray.

The increasing longing for a strong identity inside is paralleled with better control of access into the confines of the communities. By means of gates and fences, many communities regulate who can visit their communal spaces and who cannot. But even in high-end gated communities, the gates and the extensive fences at the communities' borders are not impermeable. Developers admit that gates cannot prevent intrusion or criminality within the community. But because they dissociate, they create an atmosphere of exclusivity – a feeling for the home owner of knowing who belongs and who

does not. Clearly, the gating and fencing strategies a community employs are part of the overall design concept defining an aesthetic of security. In today's communities, design and legal codes are replacing the concept of common sense that is thought to have defined the exclusivity of suburbia's public places in the past. Rarely it is more obvious that aesthetic decisions are thoroughly political.

The visual disappearance of the 'other' might be an indicator for a new tendency in the suburban unconscious. The nonidentical other becomes something beyond perception and, thus, it is no longer necessary to negotiate difference or conflict. Independent communities spring up all over the country, defining their identities mainly by design, on the basis of a total visual of sameness. The modern idea of total design has been realised where it is least expected, in suburbia, defining a new relationship between the private and public spaces inside, as well as the interior and exterior spaces.

In the case of DC Ranch, the subtle, hardly visible borders extend the idea of sameness even beyond the physical borders. Within these highly controlled environments, it is no surprise that a high percentage of confrontations between the inhabitants are about the questioning of aesthetic rules. Considering the short history of this phenomenon, we can only speculate how many people within these confines might start to ask for the reintegration of ruptures and breaks within this visual construction. Perhaps in the future, suburbia's inhabitants will long for a broadened perception of their environment rather than for total visuals. Δ

Note
1 Mark Wigley, 'Bloodstained architecture', *Post Ex Sub Dis: Urban Fragmentations and Constructions*, edited by the Ghent Urban Studies Team (GUST), 010 Publishers (Rotterdam), 2002.

Ines Schaber is an artist living in Berlin, and Jörg Stollmann is an architect teaching at the ETH Zürich and living in Zürich and Berlin. Since their studies at Princeton University in 1999, they have worked together on the Reservoirs project. On Movers and Shapers (Schaber/Stollmann) and Celebration (Schaber) are two projects resulting from this research.

11

Above
We are looking east to the mountains that are part of the community's property. Here, we see a blending of landscaping zones that is typical at the fringes of the project. In the foreground, a future transitional zone blends into a natural character zone, which finally blends into the untouched, presumably preserved desert. Only a small piece of the golf course's green lawn appears at the foothill of the mountains.

Orange County China. Or the Genius Loci of Suburbia in the Age of Global Capitalism

As millions of Chinese continue to migrate from the impoverished countryside into the cities in an attempt to improve their living conditions, a new countertrend is emerging: attracted by advertising images of affluent Western lifestyles, wealthy city-dwellers are starting to buy villas outside the immediate metropolitan areas. **Barbara Münch** describes what happens when Chinese investors clone southern Californian suburbia and doctor it onto Beijing's periphery.

It feels incredibly good to escape the crowded, smoggy city. As we drive north, the mountains get closer and closer, we are surrounded by green fields and the air becomes crystal clear. Using the new motorway, we leave Beijing – this moloch with about 10 million inhabitants[1] – quickly behind us. After only half an hour's driving we can see two 'villages' from the elevated highway, just next to each other, and about the same size. The first has row after row of small red-brick houses with curved, grey-tiled roofs, typical of the villages around Beijing. However, it has a strange neighbour – a perfect piece of 'American Suburbia' seems to have been implanted in this arid rural landscape. It consists of Mediterranean-style homes

the mountains in the north and the Wenyu river directly south of the site, a previous investor had failed to develop the area because of its distance from the city. Therefore, after acquiring the land, Yang Deng and his boss, Zhang Bo, visited Japan, Germany and the US searching for a new concept that could make their risky project a success. Orange County, in California, is where they found what they were looking for. Says Yang Deng: 'It is the American way of life that suits China best: large open living and dining areas, lots of bathrooms and a great variety of luxury private homes in different classical styles.'

This is in complete contrast to the Chinese housing of the Mao era, but is the dream of the Chinese newly rich who are willing – and able – to spend between $225,000 and $1.3 million for one of the 162 Italian-,

Opposite
Guards patrol the unfrequented streets between the 'Italian-, Spanish- and French-style' dream homes. Not many of the owners, whose main residences are usually apartments in the city, seem to have come out here to their second homes this weekend.

Above
Young workers concentrate on getting the 'urban' paths-network in Orange County China straight, preparing the ground for the third phase, which is just being constructed, thereby enlarging the walled implant eastwards into the rural surroundings.

cramped together in a strangely dense way. A high wall that surrounds the houses seemingly prevents them from spreading out into the vast, undeveloped countryside.

Undeveloped countryside? Yang Deng, the vice president of SinoCEA, the developer of Orange County China, awaits us at the heavily guarded gates of the community and explains that most of the land around Beijing has now been sold and plans for its development are ready. He admits that his site is quite far out, but explains that this is the reason why Orange County China got there in the first place. Although the surroundings are beautiful, with

French- or Spanish-style 'American homes' in Orange County. 'Nothing special,' explains Jenny Lin, editor of lifestyle magazine *Trends Home*, 'some villas in Beijing are sold for over $2 million; $500,000 is not expensive. There are quite a few people who can afford that, including many of our readers.'

However, the average salary of a full-time worker in Beijing is around $210 a month, and this is umpteen times the salary of China's underemployed rural population. While the latter therefore migrate to the cities in the millions to try their luck, a growing group of city dwellers seeks to distinguish themselves from the masses through exclusivity and lifestyle. It is this group that Orange County China targets. Most of the new

People are happy if they still have a secure job – a seven-day week and 12-hour work day are not at all unusual. And they can only hope to get their seven days' official annual leave each year and save money to buy a flat in one of the numerous apartment blocks mushrooming everywhere.

home-owners are businesspeople or artists, some of whom have just returned from abroad.

But whatever happened to China? Every good communist would see in this project the ultimate perfection of Western decadence, capitalist exploitation and profit-seeking imperialism. But over the last two decades China's cities have experienced a real revolution under the ideological cover of modest reform. This has included the privatisation of economic life and the segregation of society – the development of social classes as well as the pluralisation of lifestyles and value systems.

While in the mid-1970s uniformity reigned in the form of blue Mao-suits with standard haircuts, the majority of the academic elite was forced to work in people's communes in the countryside, and many Chinese in general were still fighting for survival, today Manchester capitalism has set out to conquer China. People are happy if they still have a secure job – a seven-day week and 12-hour work day are not at all unusual. And they can only hope to get their seven days' official annual leave each year and save money to buy a flat in one of the numerous apartment blocks mushrooming everywhere.

However, even these blocks no longer have anything in common with the standardised housing blocks of the Maoist era. Instead, they try to compete for the attention of potential customers with pseudo-classical facades, Euro-style decoration or large Chinese roofs. The average floor area per person has risen from 3.6 square metres at the beginning of the reforms in 1978 to 50 square metres in the new apartment buildings in Beijing today. Even the average citizen can buy a flat with several bathrooms and huge living rooms which, at the same time, serve as representative entrance halls.

This seems to be the counter-reaction to the crowded living conditions of former times, when most of daily life was limited to one room and you could call yourself lucky if you had a lavatory of your own. While 10 years ago the main topic of conversation with friends was whether or not to buy a colour TV or a fridge, today it is the purchase of a new flat. Thus, the demand for newly built living space is booming – and so is the property market.

As in other parts of the world, the young capitalism here has not had time to develop its own value system and therefore draws on the status symbols of the West, and especially the US. Consequently, in recent years the 'villa' has become one of the symbols of affluence, status and style. More and more property developers

build dream homes, huge 'classical American villas' for people who are about to own a house for the first time in their life and, thus, do not really know what criteria to use. In principle the designs of all these homes follow the same requirements and appeal to the same dreams as do the new apartment blocks. Just like these, they offer all the luxury that their potential buyers had to do without for such a long time. In a way, the 'villas' merely represent the next step up the status ladder, as ownership of a large apartment is no longer anything special. Since the newly rich are keen to show off their newly acquired position and lifestyle, porticos and huge reception halls are common. Actually , most of these homes look like inflated copies of the houses in the film *The Truman Show*, a mixture of American country house and European colonial-style villa.

It is also very important that there is a special room for any imaginable function, neither a clubroom, wine cellar, room for home cinema, bar or fitness room (in the basement), nor a Chinese and an American kitchen, a library, studio, and so on should be missing. Ideally, every bedroom has its own large bathroom. Another must is at least one garage, although garages are sometimes converted into accommodation for the maid and the car is parked in front of the house instead. In this way the other 'good' rooms can be used for guests instead of being 'wasted' on the maid from the countryside.

Houses are mostly very deep compact volumes contrary to their American counterparts, in order to achieve maximum building area in terms of square metres on the given small plots of land. Land resources in China are scarce and land-use rights are costly.[2] This is also one of the reasons why gardens are generally surprisingly small for such luxury homes so far out of the city. Orange County is no exception in all these respects. With regard to the size of the gardens, Yang explains that for the Chinese this doesn't really matter. The desolate state of most of the small existing gardens confirms his statements. 'The Chinese new home-owner has neither time nor interest for gardening.' In a society where a minority has just escaped from the rural past, and where the fresh air of the countryside seems to be enjoyable by the newly rich only in this well-guarded way, cut off from real country life, gardening is still regarded not as a pleasant spare-time activity but as work for farmers. Therefore, only the public areas of Orange County are really well looked after by the many employees of the compound.

Despite growing individualism, the whole idea of living outside the city in one's own house is still quite offbeat for Chinese urban dwellers. Even though all of the new home-owners who can afford to buy one of the colonial-style homes in Orange County China also have one or more cars, they cannot really imagine living so far out permanently without urban infrastructure, urban

Top
The large billboard-walls that crisscross the community are not advertisements, but are intended to help create the exquisite Western flair Orange County China promises in this wintry countryside north of Beijing.

Middle
The only public facility within the high-class gated community is this inconspicuous container-box that houses a small grocery store, where a young woman just 'drives in' to buy some drinks. Home owners will usually bring everything they need for their stay from the city.

Bottom
At first sight, just the Chinese flag hints at the true location of this 'placeless' central square. Despite the nice day, the square is deserted, just like the rest of the development, inhabited only by a few black cars with dark mirrored windows.

Opposite, top
This outdated site model survived in storage. The dense, more urban housing in the left corner will not be built. On the right, where the model still shows a landscaped public park, the third phase of Orange County's American-style homes is instead under construction.

Opposite, bottom
Only a few hundred metres away from Orange County China is another 'village' of about the same size. Here, market life is bustling; all kinds of daily necessities from food to haircuts are sold in the public space of the street.

neighbourhood and urban schools. More than 90 per cent of them are second home-buyers, also having an apartment in the city. Occasionally, certain family members live temporarily in these new homes, but they are mostly used as weekend and holiday homes, or to invite friends over to appreciate the owner's success story. To meet this latter criterion, the homes first have to reach the necessary value of prestige. And this is exactly the horse the developers of Orange County China bet on – and did very well.

Competing with the many similar American-, European- or whatever style villa-compounds[3] mushrooming around Beijing, the developers of Orange County China decided to try to come as close as possible to the American original, in order to distinguish themselves from the others. They hired the American architectural firm Bassenian Lagoni, American landscape designer Seamon, Whiteside and Associates, and American interior-design company Ambrosia. They built a number of model homes where everything, including the design, construction wood and interior finishes such as furniture, dishes and pictures on the wall, was imported. The model homes are equipped with large open-floorplan dining areas and Western-style kitchens, where Italian still-lifes out of pasta, pesto and garlands of garlic create a 'Mediterranean' atmosphere. The walls are decorated with Western tapestry and the boards of the imitation fireplaces with

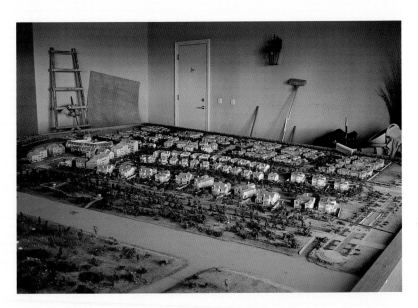

They built a number of model homes, where everything, including the design, construction wood and interior finishes such as furniture, dishes and pictures on the wall, was imported.

golden-framed photographs showing Western couples and children.

This Orange County model seems to be very successful. Only at the beginning did the developers have some problems selling the large 760- to 840-square-metre villas on the riverside. In contrast to the smaller homes, which sold extremely well, these $1.3 million houses were still quite high-priced for the young Chinese market with its limited purchasing power. Ironically, it was the outbreak of the SARS epidemic that helped the investors, as people who could afford it tried to escape the city and their apartment blocks, with the result that within a few weeks all of the luxury villas had been sold. Today, with the economy steadily growing, the market for 'villas' is rapidly expanding. Therefore, the third phase of Orange County Beijing is under construction and the developers, together with

Right
Looking north along the street that connects Orange County China directly with Beijing. On the right is the 'American Suburban Design' implant. On the left, across the river, is a traditional village hidden behind the trees. In the foreground, local peasants wait for the bus to town to sell their products. Whereas the inhabitants of Orange County China were happy to turn their backs on the city, these villagers dream of finding work there to escape rural underemployment, and to be able to buy one of the new flats in the endless housing estates being built on the edges of Beijing.

the architects Bassenian Lagoni, are planning further Orange Counties near other major Chinese cities, like Shanghai and Chengdu.

It is interesting that it does not seem to matter at all to the inhabitants that they live in a perfectly set-up copy from another world, actually in one of numerous multiple copies, with little individual touch. In fact, all of the homes are a Chinese version of an American adaptation of a European-style villa that is then multiplied a few hundred times on the same site – even on different sites in the country – that all look more or less the same. The explanation is straightforward. The notion of 'copy' in China simply lacks the pejorative connotations that it inevitably stirs within a Western cultural context. For hundreds of years the act of building did not thrive on innovation but on strict rules handed on from one generation to the next. Architecture was nothing but an instrument to express social order. Everything from the height of the building and the number of columns, to the choice of colours was used to symbolise and consolidate the existing hierarchical structure of society.

Chinese classic architecture, just like Chinese classic art, has developed in the form of a succession of copies with minor changes over time. Still today, the attitude 'Why not copy something that has been proved to be good', is very common. And in this way one can at least be sure not to make a wrong choice, but to keep up with the trend. Where Westerners often see yawning monotony, the Chinese feel assured in their decision by the synonymous choices of their fellow home-buyers. They clearly do not see the imported peace as alien to their lives, as Yang makes clear above when he says that it is exactly the American way of life that fits the Chinese best. By the beginning of the 20th century the German sinologist August Conrady had already identified a 'power of amalgamation inherent in Chinese culture, that allows to transform the foreign according to its own taste and to use its material'.[4]

A closer look at Orange County China reveals its hybrid character. As Yang admits, most Chinese customers still replace the originally wooden American homes with a concrete version which is not only cheaper but, in their eyes, also more solid. They also prefer to decorate their homes with local interior finishes, for economic reasons. Although Spanish-, French- or Italian-looking from the outside, the interior floorplans of the American homes have been altered according to Chinese requirements. Orientation is a particularly important criteria.[5] Due to the extremely hot summer sun, south orientation is preferred to west. Contrary to Western customs, the master bedroom must always face south, and in addition a tiny Chinese kitchen with a gas stove for wok-cooking must be provided in order to avoid the heavy oily fumes getting

Top
Seen from the neighbouring
traditional village, Orange
County China seems as far
away as Orange County
California on the other side of
the Pacific. And yet, physically,
just one road separates them,
a distance that only the
servants of the gated new
home-owners overcome,
sometimes in order to buy
fresh vegetables in the market
streets of the village.

Bottom
Standing south of the Wenyu
river looking north onto the
large, luxury $1.3 million
riverside villas of Orange
County, lined up in a strangely
dense way behind a wall in the
still vastly undeveloped
countryside.

Opposite
Standing on the elevated
highway, the sixth ring road,
that runs eastwards along
the northern edge of both
this traditional village and
Orange County, looking
southeast onto the former.
The village is a typical example
of the rural settlements all
around Beijing, consisting of
row after row of small, single-
storey red-brick houses with
grey-tiled, slightly curved
roofs and walled front yards.

Notes
1 City and inner suburbs
(registered and estimated
floating population). The entire
Beijing municipality today has
a registered population of 14
million and an estimated total
population of about 20 million
people.
2 Land cannot be owned
privately, therefore only land-
use rights can be bought.
3 There are only very few
exceptions, like the
Community at the Great Wall,
a project even further outside
Beijing, which tries to
establish a new Chinese villa-
architecture.
4 August Conrady in WP
Wassiljew, *Die Erschlieflung
Chinas: Kulturhistorische
und wirtschaftspolitische
Aufsätze zur Geschichte
Ostasiens*, Leipzig, 1909.
5 While in summer the sun
in the south stands very
high in Beijing due to its
southern latitude and
therefore does not really
penetrate the building,
the lower afternoon sun
shines deep into the rooms
and heat them up.

into the furniture. The large, open, American-style kitchen is more for decoration.

Needless to say, it is not the owners who do the cooking, but their servants, who either come from the city with their family for the weekend or live in the 'villa' permanently to guard the house. The servants are also likely to be the only point of contact between Orange County China and its neighbouring rural village. Although villagers are not allowed to enter the compound, the servants are likely to go to the village to buy fresh ingredients, if indeed this is necessary as home owners usually bring everything they need from the city. It is therefore not surprising that Orange County China itself offers few facilities. However, a community centre in the form of a European castle is under construction. There is a swimming pool and a restaurant, and plans for further shopping facilities in the future. Until then, the only place to buy anything in Orange County China is an inconspicuous white container-box that houses a small kiosk. As we pass by it, a car stops in front of it and a young woman jumps out to buy some drinks. Although it is a nice Sunday morning, she is one of the very few people around, apart from a group of construction workers and the omnipresent blue-uniformed guards.

In complete contrast to this, after leaving the main entrance gate, where the guards give a friendly salute, we find ourselves – physically only a few hundred metres away – in the middle of bustling market life. The public space of the street is the place where all kinds of daily necessities are sold, ranging from food to haircuts. We stroll through the busy streets where large stacks of firewood are piled up, eat freshly baked waffles, and take pictures of children playing and women washing

When we ask the villagers what they think about their new neighbour, they do not really know what to say. It is just there, it has nothing to do with their lives.

clothes in a small brook. When we ask the villagers what they think about their new neighbour, they do not really know what to say. It is just there, it has nothing to do with their lives. While the people in Orange County China have fulfilled their dream of a villa in the countryside, these people dream of a different better life: perhaps a job in the city and the chance to buy one of the new flats in the endless housing estates being built on the edge of Beijing. What should they do with a weekend home in the countryside? ᴆ

Barbara Münch studied architecture at the Technical University Berlin, where she taught from 2000–02, and the Architectural Association in London. She has since been living in Beijing and Berlin, researching the production of the contemporary Chinese city. She is currently associate professor at the Beijing Institute for Civil Engineering and Architecture.

Strategic Sprawl: Suburbanisation as Warfare in the Occupied West Bank

In the West Bank, strategies developed for military fortification and the claiming of territories have infiltrated civil planning. More surprising, perhaps, is how powerful a tool suburban development has proved to be at the hands of the Israeli authorities. The London- and Tel Aviv-based architect Eyal Weizman has analysed, both independently, in conjunction with the Israeli human rights organisation B'Tselem and together with Rafi Segal, the prevailing planning and architectural strategies as an infringement of international and human rights. Through a substantial email dialogue with Weizman, guest-editors **Ilka and Andreas Ruby** discussed with him how systematic suburbanisation has played such an effective role in Israel's claiming of authority over this contested territory.

Throughout its history, the state of Israel has used the strategic placement of settlements as a means to formulate its claims over territories that have been outside its internationally agreed borders since the 1967 war. Over the past few decades the nature of these settlements has undergone a crucial paradigm shift. Whereas Labour governments produced mainly kibbutz- and moshav-type settlements – self-sustained agricultural collectives with a strong emphasis on a shared social life among its members – the conservative Likud party, which came into power in 1977, promoted a new suburban typology of settlement. This has resulted in the so-called 'community settlement', a dormitory enclave of single-family houses that are placed, without any local economy, on the hilltops of the occupied territories of the West Bank.

The recent suburbanisation of the West Bank remains difficult, if not incomprehensible, for an outsider to understand. It is a clear-cut inversion that Weizman was able to explain in terms of Ariel Sharon's rise as a military leader and his consequent transfer to the political realm:

'This paradigm shift was generated out of a military/strategic shift in thinking about fortifications and resonated in emerging civilian planning practices. The politics of the Labour governments since the creation of the state sought to mark out the edges of the territories under its control with peripheral, self-sustained agricultural settlements and development towns. Termed by David Ben Gurion "the organic wall", they were built adjacent to the political borders of the state, sometimes only dozens of metres away from the international boundary lines.

'This line-based concept for the demarcation and defence of the territory fell into a profound crisis during the fortification of the Suez Canal prior to the Yom Kippur war of 1973. Ariel Sharon, being a prominent military general at the time, and already affiliated with the political right, was at the centre of this territorial debate. As early as the 1970s he forcefully argued against the fortification concept that invested itself in the linear defences constructed along the very edge of the Suez Canal. Instead of the static defence the so-called Bar Lev line afforded, he argued for, and finally built, a defence system based on the idea of a deep dynamic matrix. Spread across the hilltops throughout the depth of the Sinai desert, he erected isolated fortified strongholds and connected them with a spiking lattice of roads. If linear defence is rendered useless after being breached at a single point, a defensive matrix,

when attacked, may become flexible and adaptable to the fall of any number of single nodes by forming new connections across its depth. The proof for the superiority of the matrix over the line was given during battle when the static linear fortifications of the Bar Lev line were breached within hours of the Egyptian attack. Sharon's matrix held off a further attack and, furthermore, became the base from which his division managed to penetrate Egyptian lines.

'However, the trauma of the Egyptian breach of the Bar Lev line, and the heavy losses of the Yom Kippur war, generated a public outrage in Israel. The Golda government was replaced, but Sharon, perceived as the man who won the battle, managed to translate his popularity into political capital. Then, when the conservative Likud party came to power in May 1977 and he took over the ministerial committee in charge of settlement, Sharon was given the first opportunity to adapt the military spatiality of a dynamic battlefield into political strategy.

'Sharon saw, in the depth of the West Bank, heavily populated by Palestinians, a defensible frontier – a border without a line, across whose depth, around and between Palestinian towns and villages, a matrix of settlement, acting as civilian strongholds, would be constructed. In effect he tried to do in the West Bank, with civilian planning, what he did in the Sinai desert with military fortifications.

Opposite
The settlement of Nili, Jerusalem region. This suburban settlement is one of the prime real estates in the West Bank, its residents – typically middle-class employees in the service industry in Tel Aviv – commute to work in 40 minutes.

Right
The Mizpe Dani (top) and Horesh Yaron (bottom) outposts, West Bank. Outposts like these are quickly transported on site either by trucks or helicopters. Relocation usually means just relocation to another site – sometimes with direct advice from the authorities.

All captions throughout this article are adapted from the photograph series 'The Battle for the Hilltops', Rafi Segal and Eyal Weizman, 'Territories', Kunstwerke, Berlin, 2003.

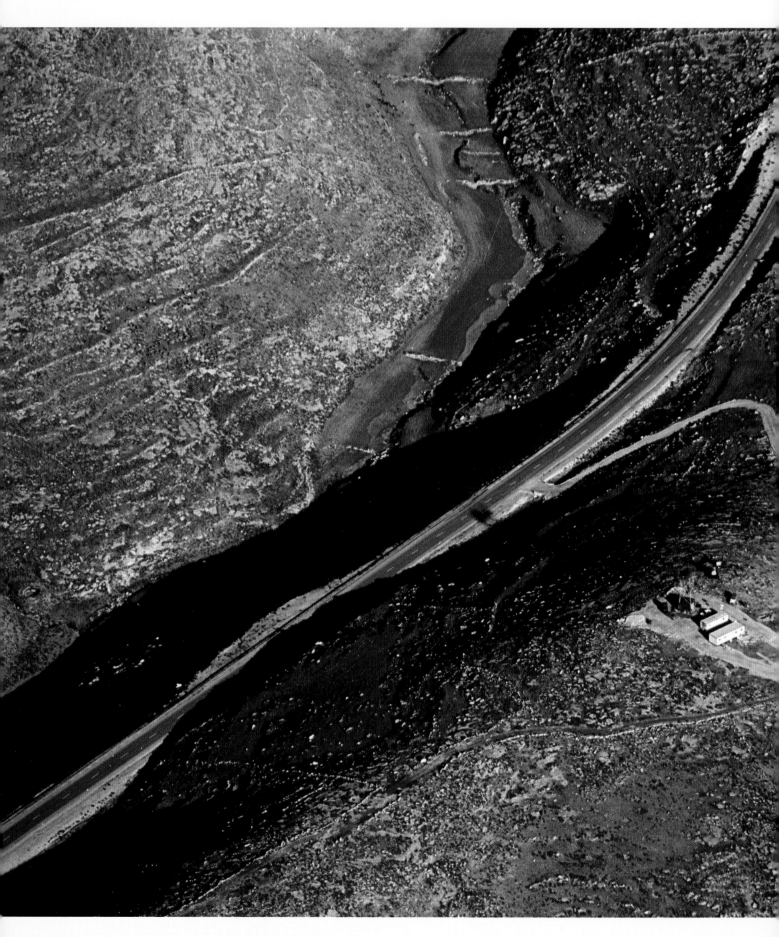

Above
Asa'el outpost, Hebron region. The outpost now comprises five caravans. These are home to four bachelors and one couple who settled in search of a secluded place to worship and live 'close to the land'. The eastern ring-road of Hebron mountain blocks Palestinian and Bedouin expansion towards the east and the shores of the Dead Sea.

'In order to populate his matrix of strongholds with civilian communities, he channelled two centrifugal forces that marked the Israeli political landscape of the late 1970s. He combined the pressures of the emerging messianic-religious impulses to settle a mythological landscape with the desire of the middle classes to push outside of congested city centres. After the Yom Kippur war, there was an upheaval of religious fundamentalism in Israel, most particularly exemplified by the national religious organisation Gush Emunim (the Block of Faith). Its ideology fused together disparate and contradictory threads that existed within Zionism: religiousness, nationalism, militarism and messianism and, above all, a fundamental belief in the completeness and sanctity of the "Land of Israel", one to be exercised through the act of settlement.

'While the settlements initiated by Gush Emunim in the central mountain ridge area were ideological, the not necessarily ideological public was drawn to the settlements that offered an improved standard of living based on large financial incentives.[1]

'Thus, by appealing to different branches of the Israeli public, ideology was sold to the ideological, religious sites to the religious, and quality of life to the middle classes. Given that settlers work in the metropolitan centres of Tel Aviv and Jerusalem, the military strategy laid out for mobile defence in depth could be perfectly used by Israeli suburbia. A massive system of 50 highways together with a modern matrix of infrastructure became effective instruments of development – merging the needs of a sprawling suburbia with national security and political ambitions to push ever-more Israelis into the West Bank. Thus, the settlement project of the West Bank managed to redraw the image of the pioneers; no longer are they the heroic agricultural settlers/soldiers but the suburban middle-class family. Suburbia became the frontier pushing new single-family houses and gardens on into "new territories", continuing the Zionist revolution.'

What is interesting from both an architectural and urban point of view is the way that the strategic staging of suburbia in the Israeli–Palestinian conflict has inversed all the usual characteristics attributed to suburbia in a Western capitalist cultural setting. If in Europe and the US the planning of suburbia is almost totally controlled by the property development market, in Israel it is planned by the state, with military ambitions (when Sharon devised the master plan for the (sub)urbanisation of the West Bank in 1982, he did so as the Israeli minister of defence). Paradoxically, the extreme land consumption by low-density building fabric, which is normally considered one of suburbia's most severe problems, seems to become one of its greatest 'virtues' under the specific circumstances of the West Bank. With this in mind, we asked Weizman to expand further on the way that the nature of urbanity and sub-urbanity had been seized and applied strategically in an Israeli context:

Top
Shaqed, Jenin region. The 'ideal' layout for a small settlement is a circle. The public functions are generally located within the innermost ring, on the highest ground. Socially, the 'community settlement' is in effect an exclusive members' club with a long admissions process and monitoring mechanism that regulates everything from religious observance through ideological rigour, and even the form and outdoor use of homes. The application of Jordanian land law throughout the occupied territories means that settlements could not be built on cultivated land; the expansion of a settlement could thus effectively be blocked by maintaining Palestinian fields around it, as shown on the bottom right of this image.

'Urbanity became the Palestinian "weapon" of retaliation, threatening to undermine the "other" urbanity of the settlements that was being produced to maintain Israeli territorial control.'

'Suburbia in the West Bank is indeed a highly effective tool in the organisation of the territory. And it was so all the more when the frictions between Palestinians and Israelis intensified, with the first *intifadah* beginning in 1987. The challenges faced by the state arose less from a conventional attack by Arab armour from the "outside" and more from a disgruntled and restless Palestinian population located "inside" the occupied territories. The centres and headquarters of popular resistance were deep within Palestinian towns and cities. In the eyes of the state these overdense and underserviced urban environments became the "habitat of terror". Palestinian urban growth, fuelled by a rapidly increasing population, "illegally" sprawled beyond their planning boundaries. Urbanity became the Palestinian "weapon" of retaliation, threatening to undermine the "other" urbanity of the settlements that was being produced to maintain Israeli territorial control.

'The way to contain these urban threats, from the perspective of Ariel Sharon's planners, was to use the weapon of counter-urbanity or, more precisely, sub-urbanity. Beyond their status as forward positions in the defence of the state from invasion, the settlements were used to allow the state to exercise the task of civilian control. A continuous fabric of homes, industrial zones and roads were knitted together to act as wedges separating the different Palestinian population centres. Homes, like armoured divisions, were used in formation across a dynamic theatre of operations to occupy strategic hills, to encircle an enemy or cut his communication lines. The location strategy employed for the West Bank was based on yet another basic military principle: the axiom that the party to move faster across a battlefield is the one to win the battle. Traffic arteries are, de facto, separated across national lines: the six-lane bypass roads on which military vehicles and civilian vans can rush between settlements contrast starkly with the narrow, informal dust-roads connecting Palestinian towns and villages.'

If the state is the de facto master planner of the suburban West Bank, it also makes one wonder whether it also acts as its master builder. There are, in fact, a number of large settlement projects that have indeed been conducted almost as a state enterprise, as they were considered of national importance. Yet, as Weizman pointed out, the community settlements in the West Bank are rarely created at once, but involve a process that passes through various stages of inhabitation:

'Most community settlements start as "outposts" – a quick urbanism of temporary homes and converted ship-containers, driven on site by track or sometimes brought in by helicopter. The founding members of a settlement live in temporary caravans. Once their permanent homes are built, the temporary homes are used to house newer arrivals or, when the influx of settlers ceases, they are altered or packed together to accommodate other small public functions.

'This can make us better understand the contemporary issue of the outposts. Almost all settlements in the West Bank began as outposts! Now, more than 120 new "temporary" outposts have been set upon the remaining strategic hilltops of the West Bank. While this method was the settlers' initiative, without approval from the relevant authorities, the government generally refrained from evicting the settlers or demolishing the buildings, while most receive retroactive approval. In a sense this points to the privatisation of politics; by pointing the blame for settling these outposts at individuals or NGOs like Gush Emunim, the government distances itself from something it sees as essential, strategically and politically, taking no blame. This apparent naivety hides the fact that, with their potential for immediacy, mobility and flexibility, these outposts are the perfect instruments of colonisation. The seed of mobile homes may then be free to transform and develop into a 'mature' settlement as conditions allow.[2]

'The temporal aspect of the outpost is thus nothing but a deceit, initially that of the government, which allowed itself to be manipulated by the settlers, and finally by the state versus the international community – in claiming a temporal aspect for these settlements.

'One must remember that occupation law, as manifested in the Hague regulations and Geneva conventions, allows temporary military modifications to an occupied land. Everything in the West Bank is argued as a temporary military need, starting with settlements (as they answer emerging strategic needs) and finishing with the barrier that is cutting through the West Bank, which again is only "temporary" until the security situation solidifies. In fact, the temporary state of emergency is what allows the occupation to exist. It's a temporary situation that will soon be 40 years old.'

The community settlements of the West Bank are sometimes very homogeneous, both in terms of their street layouts, the domestic architectural types and the clear-cut separation between the protected interior of the settlement and the 'enemy exterior' of its surrounds. This gives the impression from the outside that there was a predefined set of (suburban) typologies that have been systematically applied in the occupation settlement of the West Bank. Weizman described how, in fact, building form has been brought about by a complex dynamic driven partly by the government and partly by the internal and ideological culture of the settlers:

'In many ways, the government decision in 1978, a year after the Likud came to power, to create the first city in the West Bank, Ma'ale Edumim – a large suburb of Jerusalem, where some 25,000 people now live – was an attempt to transform the settlement project from an improvised undertaking promoted by such groups as

Above
Giveat Ha'I outpost and Psagot,
overlooking Ramallah. The
national-religious settlement of
Psagot (established 1989,
population of 1,090) is situated
on a hill within the city of
Ramallah in order to supervise
and block the eastward
development of the city.

Opposite
Ofra settlement, Ramallah
region. The form of the
mountain settlements is
constructed according to the
laws of a geometric system
that unites the effectiveness of
sight with that of spatial order,
thereby producing sight lines
that function to achieve
different forms of power:
strategic in its overlooking of
main traffic arteries,
controlling in its overlooking of
Palestinian towns and villages,
and as self-defence in
overlooking its immediate
surroundings and approach
roads. In the foreground is the
Ginot Arye Hershkowitz
outpost, and in the background
a Palestinian village.

the ideological enthusiasts of Gush Emunim, into a well-thought-through and well-produced "state project". Furthermore the employment of a prestigious town-planning practice, Thomas Leitersdorf, with experience of town planning for Europeans in the Ivory Coast, alongside 12 of the more well-known architectural teams in Israel, and economic, weather and transport experts, was intended to set the standard, to become an architectural guideline and a quality bench mark for the future settlements in the mountain regions of the West Bank. Indeed, all of the teams who worked on Ma'ale Edumim later went on to build more mountain settlements according to the practice developed there.

'In *A Civilian Occupation*, Rafi Segal and I described the intensions behind the urban layout of the settlements. We showed that, in the mountain settlements, the arrangement of the homes around summits imposes on dwellers axial visibility that is oriented in two directions: out and downwards, towards the surrounding valleys where "strategic interests" highways, main junctions and Palestinian urban areas are located; and in and upwards, towards the central common area where the social life of the community is regulated.[3] The outward-facing gaze is of strategic importance, responding to military master plans that seek to seed the territories with a field of eyes, and a tactical function for its own self-protection.

'But there is another layer of complication in the relation between settlements and vision. The settlers arrive at the West Bank seeking not to overlook strategic interests, but to celebrate life closer to nature or, indeed, to sensually experience the historical and biblical landscape as part of their ideological ritual. The gaze here, as Rafi Segal and I showed, gains a political agenda manifested through aesthetics, in seeking to re-establish the relation between terrain and sacred text. At that moment a strange process of translation begins: the strategic functions and targets that were defined by the military across the landscape start to be understood as the components of the exegetical and pastoral. The stone houses of Palestinian villages, the olive terraces and the dust road, for the supervision of which settlements were installed, are turned into political and cultural signifiers.

'A gap is opened between what the master plan, or the government, wanted settlers to see (sites of national strategic importance), what the settlers think they see (a pastoral biblical landscape) and what settlers really see (the daily life of Palestinians and their poverty under occupation).[4] The inward-facing gaze does have a reformist and conformist function; it aims to create a sense of community and regulate and control acceptable public behaviour. This gaze aims to create the settler. It is part of a series of mechanisms and apparatuses, most nonspatial that create and sustain ideological structures through the reproduction of the rituals of everyday life.

settlements in the West Bank and Gaza Strip as one of its most closely guarded secrets, and the state budget was constructed in a way that makes this information opaque.

In the most comprehensive audit of this issue conducted at the end of 2003, the Israeli newspaper *Haaretz* claimed that the additional cost of the settlements project had passed $10 billion since 1967. Accordingly, the ministry of housing and construction typically grants $5,000 to buy a flat beyond the green line and a loan of up to a further $15,000, half of which is converted into a grant, after 15 years. The ministry of national infrastructure gives a 50 per cent reduction in development costs and/or 69 per cent discount on the leasehold fees. So far, the state has spent $2.2 billion on housing, $500 million of which during one year – 1992 – when Ariel Sharon was the minister of housing in the last Shamir government.

In addition, the ministry of education provides a discount of 90 per cent for tuition fees in kindergartens, plus other benefits. The ministry of trade and industry provides favourable conditions to industry, with grants of up to 30 per cent of financing needs, as well as income tax benefits on income from the enterprise. The ministry of finance provides a 7 per cent discount in the payment of income tax. Beyond this, more money is transferred to the local authorities. Despite the fact that the settlements are generally well-off suburban communities, much stronger economically than the average population in Israel, the per capita financial transfers of the government to local authorities in the West Bank is 2.25 times higher than within Israel.
2 The logic of their creating is sometimes based on a tragic narrative of 'victimisation', where outposts are positioned over a place where a Jewish settler was murdered. A stone is then erected as a central monument, and the homes are laid in a ring around it. The murder thus becomes the rite of creation for a settlement.

On other occasions the process is purely comical, as with the outpost of Migron in the southern part of the West Bank. After refusal by the government to set up a settlement where they wanted it, a few settlers asked a mobile phone provider to build a new antenna over the hilltop, pretending reception was bad. The antenna needed a guard, housed in a mobile home, but the guard was religious and could only pray with a Talmudic *minyan* of 10 other religious

The "community settlement", being a closed-off, dead-ended cul-de-sac envelope, helped promote a shared formal and behavioural identity, and facilitated the intimate management of the lives of the inhabitants.

'The legal framework of the settlement is a cooperative association managed by its inhabitants through general meetings. The settlement absorbs new members after a clearly defined process, at the end of which the general meeting decides whether or not to accept the candidates. A member can also be expelled for not complying with group regulations after several warnings. This legal organisation of community settlements as cooperative associations capable of choosing their members, aimed to solve another difficulty imagined by state planners: How could the government avoid the eventuality that Palestinians, citizens of the Israeli state, might move to the settlements? The cooperative settlements are, in effect, closed members' clubs, with long admission processes and monitoring mechanisms that regulate everything from religious observance to ideological rigour, and even the form and outdoor use of homes.'

By virtue of their isolation from the outside world, the community settlements stir familiar images of the anti-urban escapism of the gated communities found in the US and South Africa. Given the dominance of American models in the discourse of suburbia, we were keen to find out from Weizman whether the West Bank settlements historically follow these gated communities or whether they actually precede them as a kind of suburban avant-garde.

'I think both [West Bank and gated communities] share a similar source. It is interesting to note that the settlement project is as much an offshoot of civilianised military technologies as the Levitowns of the 1950s were in America. In the US it was the military industry that started churning out line-produced homes, which were then distributed along the network of interstate highways (built to serve the US war economy). The Israeli typology of the strategic garden suburb on the hilltops was generated out of its own necessities and the particularities of the conflict, but also out of a civilianisation process (the turning of the military to the civilian, not to be mistaken with civilising, process) – a direct line from the military to civilian life. The biggest push of suburban settlements took place in the late 1970s and early 1980s. These were years during which the US experienced the beginning

of its own gating and movements such as "new urbanism" as the next stages of American suburbanisation. The climb up the West Bank mountains coincided with the flight of the middle classes and their "forting up" behind protective walls – both formations setting themselves against the poverty and violence of the Third Worlds they have produced.

'The influence of US urbanism on the West Bank is manifested along two very different and seemingly contradicting channels – the gated suburbia and the frontier. The hybrid of these two American influences – whose agents were ideologically committed immigrants from the US – mixed a somewhat Hollywood-type interpretation of life at the frontier within suburban settings. The frontier and the gated community are not as far apart as they seem – as a matter of fact, across the American frontier there are a variety of highly religious, utopian, enclosed communities with names such as "Harmony" and "Mutual Cooperation" as well as "Israel", "Palestine", "Bethlehem" and virtually every other city mentioned in the Bible, save "Sodom" perhaps. If the direction of influence runs from the American frontier to the Israeli one, experience may run the other way round. If settlements are nothing but the last, and most extreme, gesture in the urbanisation of enclaves, one that all but perfected the politics of separation and security, they could be seen as the end condition of contemporary urban and architectural

formations such as suburban enclave neighbourhoods and gated communities. Their situation today, as we hear daily in the news, may offer a possible future scenario and, indeed, a warning to what the gated communities may experience in the future. In this case the fate of the settlements must be taken seriously by anyone who is interested in the future of the suburb.'

Many observers are convinced that the conflict between Israel and Palestine can be solved only if Israel will eventually move out of the settlements in the occupied territories. There is talk that settlers might be enticed to leave behind their settlements and move to the Israeli mainland by virtue of substantial compensation payments. If we suppose, for a moment, that this scenario would become reality one day, the emptied Israeli settlements in the West Bank would, virtually overnight, touch base with the nearby Palestinian metropolitan corridors they were once built to prevent from expanding. One can think of different scenarios for these 'new satellites': they could either continue to operate as suburbia, claiming autonomy vis-à-vis their neighbouring Palestinian cities or, inversely, as Weizman explains, start to operate as their quasi-natural extension.

'Undoubtedly one of the most intriguing possibilities for us architects to think about was that raised during the failed Camp David

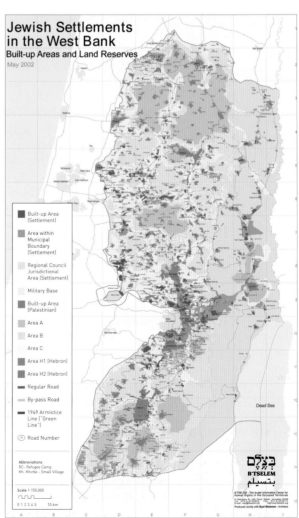

men. So 10 more mobile homes were placed there. But their families followed suit – a road was cut, a fence was built and a new settlement appeared.
3 A later architecture guideline demonstrating the experience gained in Ma'ale Edumim and in other places, advises that bedroom windows should be oriented towards the inner public spaces and the living rooms towards the distant view. This is evidence that vision has now become the primary principle of design at all scales.
4 When the architect enters the equation, the irony becomes even sharper. When Thomas Leitersdorf was interviewed by Eran Tamir for *A Civilian Occupation* (edited by Rafi Segal and Eyal Weizman, Verso Books (London), 2003), he missed this irony completely. He talked at length about his admiration for the Arab village, while designing settlements that will finally replace the village. There is hardly any settlement in the West Bank that is as harmful as Ma'ale Edumim to the prospect of creating a Palestinian state, as it literally cuts the West Bank in half.
5 The Psagot settlement is within the city of Ramallah and some 20 kilometres away from the centre of Jerusalem. The settlement of Kiryat-Arba is within Palestinian Hebron, Ariel is less than a kilometre from the Palestinian city of Salfit, and 35 kilometres away from central Tel Aviv, where its residents work; Elon Moreh is a few hundred metres from Nablus and about 50 kilometres from Tel Aviv.

negotiations in July 2000. There, Barak and Clinton proposed to Arafat that, as part of a general restitution package aimed at Palestinian refugees, the totality of real-estate and infrastructure in settlements to be evacuated – some hundred relatively small communities in remote places adjacent to Palestinian towns – be given back to the Palestinian people in exchange for the property that the refugees left behind in Israel proper. This means that some settlement-suburbs will have to be integrated into Arab towns. This incredible and hilarious transformation can be imagined if one realises that settlements can be thought of as suburban when put in relation to the Israeli cities and employment centres – at an average of 25 kilometres from them – but will be thought of as urban when put in relation to the Palestinian towns that they physically border.[5]

'Needless to say these Israeli settlement-suburbs currently have no relation to the Palestinian town, save for their desire to limit growth. By changing the central coordinate system of the settlements from Israeli to Palestinian, their suburban built fabric would have to transform completely. Initially, the negotiating parties mentioned above imagined that no Palestinian would like to live in evacuated settlements, which would thus be destroyed and pulverised. But along the way, with the liberation struggle slowly turning into a housing problem, the opposite may indeed happen.

'On the other hand, we can indulge for a moment in what the outcome of a process of *détournement* – to use the Situationist term defined as the radical liberating and critical reappropriation of existing environments – might be. Would the small-scale single-family homes be erased, converted or extruded? Would the single unit of the family home be extended on two sides to become a courtyard house? Would its red roof be painted over, removed and replaced with a flat or domed roof? Will its Jerusalem-stone cladding and stucco arches be pulled apart? Would the panoptic layout of the settlement be blocked by a haphazard spreading out of urban objects blocking its mechanism and rendering it inoffensive? Could the cul-de-sac, dead-end arrangement of homes be cut apart by two-lane through-traffic? Would the green, watered grass lawns turn into small family fields? It would be likewise telling if the synagogue would be turned into a mosque or a cinema ...

'As an architect one would like to see radical intervention – the conversion, erasure and transgression of the existing built culture of settlements, an aggression towards architecture that many sites of suburbia are so successful in generating.' ⌂

Eyal Weizman was born in Israel and studied architecture in London. He has taught at the Bartlett School of Architecture in London, University for Applied Arts in Vienna and Technion, Israel Institute for Technology in Haifa. In 2000 he started a practice in Tel Aviv with Rafi Segal. Together they curated the exhibition 'A Civilian Occupation – The Politics of Israeli Architecture' that was due to be shown at the UIA in Berlin in 2002 but cancelled for political reasons. With Israeli human rights organisation B'Tselem, Weizman has developed a study of prevailing architecture and planning strategies in the West Bank as an infringement of international and human rights.

The *Barriadas* of Lima: Utopian City of Self-Organisation?

Organised by groups of migrants from rural areas, the invasion of public territory and its occupation by self-constructed dwellings is the most frequent path to suburban development in Peru. Since the state is not able to provide housing for these migrants, it tolerates their acts of claiming territory and post-legalises the informal settlements, which over time become consolidated. Taking us to the desert periphery of Lima, **Kathrin Golda-Pongratz** describes the foundation, development and organisation of these *barriadas*.

'When dwellers control the major decisions and are free to make their own contributions in the design, construction, or management of their housing, both this process and the environment produced stimulate individual and social well-being.'
— John FC Turner[1]

In August 1963, the British architect John F Charlewood Turner guest-edited an issue of *Architectural Design* issue on 'Dwelling Resources in South America', focusing on the *barriadas* of Lima. Forty years later, by recalling the importance of his commitment, another look at the Peruvian self-made cities evokes a number of questions: How have the *barriadas* developed since then? What kinds of cities are they? What are their peculiar characteristics? What is their contemporary urban role? And how do people live in these settlements at the beginning of the 21st century?

The Peruvian capital today seems to be a never-ending city extending itself along the coastline, growing further north and south into the so-called Cono Norte and Cono Sur along the milestones of the Pan-American Highway, before fading out into the desert. Innumerable buses, microbuses and collective taxis in the city centre take one out to the periphery, conductors yelling all kinds of destinations with promising names like Ciudad de Diós or Villa El Salvador, or names of Andean places, which in Lima represent peripherial urbanisations.

The road to Villa El Salvador is long, and the microbus mostly overcrowded as it passes stop-and-go through the congested and noisy centre, along the small industrial and residential barrios (Spanish-speaking communities) of La Victoria and Lince, through the new high-rise financial centre of San Isidro, the elegant Miraflores and the bohemian Barranco. It stops wherever passengers want to get on or off, rushes further out to the rhythm of *chicha* music,[2] passing by huge military areas, commercial centres and industrial plants. The desert is covered with a carpet-like grid of small sheds and houses as far as the eye can see. The colours are light and soft, mixed with different tones of the grey of the foggy sky and the desert sand.

The young town of Villa El Salvador begins around 30 kilometres south of Lima's centre. Schools, small industry, a radio station, social clubs and flat houses built of bricks and concrete with small gardens line wide streets where noisy mototaxis speedily take one further into the different sectors of the town. Along the busy main streets, the colourful facades of grocery stores, tailors, craft shops, hairdressers, little restaurants, Internet cafés and workshops make it hard to believe that some 30 years ago life here began with an invasion of desert dunes.

Thus becomes clear the strength of the immigrants' determination to make the desert their own, to establish new roots and networks, and to transform inhospitable territories into their places of life – a solidarity and firm belief in the *barriada* as an urban opportunity. The existence of the occupied sand hills further out is evidence that this will is still there, that people keep on starting a new life in a rush-mat shed on desert lands within the metropolitan area, in the hope of becoming citizens.

Migration and the Emergence of Suburban Settlements

Migration of rural populations to Lima has determined life in Peru since the 1940s. Today almost a third of the 27 million Peruvians live in greater Lima, and about 75 per cent of its citizens are immigrants; 40 per cent of the capital's 7.8 million inhabitants live in the more or less consolidated informal city.[3]

The dominance of the capital and the roots of centralism date back to colonial times, when Lima was the seat of the Spanish political and ecclesiastical power and a centre of culture, knowledge and civilisation. This notion, and the promise of opportunities, mark cultural and social values in contemporary Peru, accompanied by a certain unease about the grey and tough metropolis *Lima la horrible*.[4]

Progress, health care, education, employment and the promise of better living conditions draw people from the rural communities to the capital. The social and economic marginalisation of Selvatic[5] and Andean territories, natural disasters like earthquakes, landslides and the consequences of the *Fenómeno del Niño* in the late 1990s, resulted in internal migration. Agrarian reform failed in the 1970s, and the terrorism of the Maoist Shining Path movement (*Sendero Luminoso*), and the violent counteraction of the military forces and police, determined the 1980s and 1990s and caused the dislocation of tens of thousands of sierra

inhabitants, especially from the Ayacucho area and Central Highlands, between 1988 and 1992.

Lima's immediate surroundings were affected by a first wave of immigration in the early 1940s, simultaneous with the installation of modern infrastructure and industry in the capital. In 1946, informal settlements emerged on the San Cosme hill, its proximity to the recently built new central market being a magnet for *campesinos* hoping to find work. The aspiration for modernisation and the incessant urban growth as phenomena of mutual stimulation and constant conflict have since marked Lima's development.

The dominant white and mestizo population was intolerant of the acquisition of land by Indian migrants, and slum clearance programmes threatened inner-city dwellers with the loss of their living space in central *tugurios*.[6] However, the migrant invasion of uncultivated state territories frequently proved a viable alternative, and the government gradually came to tolerate it.[7] In the following decades, this tolerance was to become an efficient political instrument.

The 1990s was a decade of massive land invasions, each time reaching territories more inadequate for urban use. In the mid-1990s, around 700 clandestine occupations emerged in Lima, and 14 mayoral ones between 1998 and 2002. In quantitative terms, invasion of public territory and self-construction is responsible for the majority of city and housing development in Peru.[8]

Invasion Strategies and *Barriada* Politics

Through a massive invasion of the San Juan desert on Christmas Eve in 1954, overnight the Ciudad de Diós (City of God) *barriada* was created. Organised families built up a satellite town following the traditional rules of a Spanish–Andean symbiosis: along the existent Atocongo road they subdivided the desert into regular plots between 24 and 100 square metres, and traced streets and a plaza where a cinema, hospital, shops and a church were installed. As a result, the ministry of housing was forced to distribute titles of property to more than 100,000 settlers.[9]

It is striking to see to what extent these new spontaneous settlements identify with traditional urban patterns dating back to the early days of Peruvian colonial history. In the early 16th century, the Spanish Leyes de Indias imposed on Peruvian territories the emblematic rational chequerboard grid, which was determined neither by directions of wind nor by the laws of topography. It was open and without any spatial limitation. The structure of the colonial city foundation was anti-topographical and expandable, and it enabled Spain to systematically conquer the South American continent. The central plaza was the decisive germ from which the city would develop.[10]

This idea of the city as a rational grid structure determines the Peruvian spatial concept and is

Notes

1 From the website of the Right Livelihood Award, www.rightlivelihood.se. John FC Turner worked in Peru between 1957 and 1965, introducing and promoting self-help programmes as an employee of national government agencies. His publications have influenced housing policies worldwide. In 1977 he received the International Union of Architects' Sir Robert Matthew Prize for Architecture. He underlined the credo of the self-organised city in the 1970s and 1980s, a consequence of political reluctance and of the Habitat declaration in 1977, mentioning self-construction support as an effective method of avoiding social and political tension in metropolitan areas. In the 1990s a change in settlement politics in Latin America was initiated, according to the Second Habitat conference, which demanded the strengthening of urban and regional planning, and a global action plan for sustainable settlement development.

2 *Chicha* is a Peruvian soft drink made of black corn, sugar and citric acid. It gives its name to a new urban music style, a mixture of Latin pop and traditional folklore elements.

3 In 1956, 120,000 people lived in suburban settlements; in 1983 the authorities counted two million. Today, the population is 3.1 million. Numbers according to the National Institute of Statistics and Informatics (INEI), *Distribución de la población total por regiones naturales*, available at www.inei.gob.pe.

4 Sebastián Salazar Bondy, *Lima la horrible*, Ediciones Peisa, Biblioteca Peruana (Lima), 1962.

5 The Selva is the Peruvian tropical rainforest, which covers about 60 per cent of the country's territory.

6 *Tugurio* is the Peruvian denomination for densely populated and decaying inner-city slums.

7 Peter Lloyd, *The Young Towns of Lima: Aspects of Urbanization in Peru*,

reproduced in its spontaneous settlements. But it becomes irrational, and even destructive, where topography is fragile and microclimates and the ecological balance for the whole metropolitan zone are endangered. Such relations and ruptures, structural and social effects between the central and peripherial city, determine Lima's urban dynamics.

Finally, the Barriada Law of 1961 acknowledged unplanned occupation of public and private land in urban fringe areas,[11] and infrastructure and technical government assistance supported the self-construction process, which to the present day remains a cheap and relatively simple solution to the housing problem.[12]

For the first time, in 1971 due to a massive and violent invasion, the military government of the time planned an official settlement for 50,000 inhabitants as an example of poverty orientation, modernisation and social reformation.[13] And this is how Villa El Salvador was created. Functionaries of the SINAMOS[14] provided water, health care and transport links to Lima, and the aspiration to hierarchical social order found its spatial expression in an urbanistic form.

Since then, the reproduction of this urban prototype has been more or less instigated by the state. In 1979, areas with titled plots were denominated as *urbanizaciones populares* and had to be recognised as ordinary districts with municipal rights and responsibilities. Between 1990 and 2000, Alberto Fujimori's neoliberal dictatorial government promoted further suburban growth. Schools were built and infrastructure improved, while propaganda boards for self-construction all over the city evoked the dream of owning one's own house. As a populist instrument of power centralisation, the Commission for the Official Registration of Informal Property (COFOPRI) took over the municipalities' task of distributing land titles, and the government literally provoked invasions and social upheavals in order to resettle people in distant desertlands, to demonstrate social engagement and gain the votes of the poor.

In the young towns of today, the second and third generations of immigrants have already formed their own families. As their barrios and parents' houses become too small, they are gradually invading and urbanising vacant territories within the existing settlements; thus public space and living conditions are diminishing and *barriada* dwellers are now faced with new social and spatial challenges.

Hole Becomes Home, Tent Becomes Temple

The flat desertland around Lima, and the dry climate, favour invasion and make life in a precarious shed tolerable for months, until savings suffice to build a solid and more permanent home.

On bank holidays, when police and institutional control is low, organised families frequently occupy

Water is scarce and difficult to obtain. Until installation of a water supply, it is distributed by tanks once or twice a week and anxiously expected, especially in the summer, when children can be seen chasing after the distribution trucks.

suburban territories and erect the Peruvian flag on their plots. After 24 hours without official intervention, the land is declared and taken. (In contrast, early invaders dug holes in the sand on the outskirts of Lima to define the first steps of settlement.) Initially, materials such as cardboard, wooden fruit-boxes and plastic are collected or bought with minimal investment to secure the plot and provide a minimum of shelter. Meanwhile, a whole industry of basic building materials including wooden piles and rush mats (*esteras*) emerges on the edges of the Pan-American Highway.

The process of consolidation depends on political interests and the capacity for self-organisation and solidarity among the dwellers. There is a close relation between official registrations of property and standards of living. Settlements undergo several phases of construction, from cane or cheap wood shelters to houses of noble materials such as brick or concrete. Building materials and architectural styles are a clear manifestation of social status, and the upgrading dweller imitates the wealthy barrios or the kind of international architecture seen on television. Architecture is ambivalent, modern as well as traditional, and temporal as houses are never finished, forms and materials change, and the use of rooms is often not specified: for example, the garage may be turned into a shop and the hall into a workshop.[15]

Infrastructure is initially self-organised. Transport is the first system to be organised, in an informal network of microbuses and collective taxis, in order to reach places of importance such as markets, authorities and jobs in the consolidated city. The dry climate helps to maintain unpaved access roads until, as part of its formalisation process, the government provides paving.

Water is scarce and difficult to obtain. Until installation of a water supply, it is distributed by tanks once or twice a week and anxiously expected, especially in summer, when children can be seen chasing after the distribution trucks. Many *barriadas* situated in the highest zones of hill settlements still do not have running water after years of existence and pay a twentyfold price for it. However, since the privatisation of the respective companies in the 1990s, private and public electricity, water, sewage and telephone connections are now installed more rapidly. Around 60 per cent of houses have electricity, 30 per cent have water and 18 per cent a sewerage system.

The horizontal growth of the suburbs elevates the cost of infrastructure enormously. Here, vertical *barriada* densification could be a solution. As state credit is too poor to run such projects efficiently, nongovernmental organisations (NGOs) provide technical advice and international support. In Villa El Salvador, the NGOs Desco and Provipo try to break people's refusal to live in multistorey houses and rent rooms to non-family members.

Cambridge University Press,
(Cambridge), 1980, p 5.
8 Carlos Escalante, 'Towards
decentralized housing
improvement policies in Peru',
*Trialog 78, Social Production
of Habitat in Latin America*,
Iko-Verlag (Frankfurt am
Main), 2003, p 16f.
9 Analysed in Josè Matos Mar,
Las Barriadas de Lima 1957,
2nd edn, Instituto de Estudios
Peruanos (Lima), 1977, p 93ff.
10 In the case of Lima, the
original plan of 117 *cuadras*
was partly adjusted to pre-
Hispanic paths. See Kathrin
Golda-Pongratz, 'Struktur-
und Bedeutungswandel des
Zentrums einer
iberoamerikanischen
Metropole. Städtebauliche
Ideen und Perspektiven der
Raumentwicklung in Lima
1940–2000', doctoral thesis,
Institute for Urban and
Regional Planning, University
of Karlsruhe, unpublished
document, p 7.
11 Julio Calderón Cockburn,
'Official Registration
(Formalization) of Property in
Peru (1996–2000)', conference
at ESF/N-AERUS international
workshop in Leuven and
Brussels, Belgium, May 2001.
12 Further details can be
found in Eberhard Kross, *Die
Barriadas von Lima.
Stadtentwicklungsprozesse in
einer lateinamerikanischen
Metropole*, Schöningh Verlag
(Paderborn), 1992.
13 In 2003, Villa El Salvador
counted 388,000 inhabitants
with a density of 9.2
inhabitants per square
kilometre.
14 Sistema Nacional de Apoyo a
la Movilización Social (SINAMOS)
was a state organisation set up
to mobilise the population
during the military government
of General Juan Velasco
Alvarado (1968–75), who was
followed by General Francisco
Morales Bermúdez.
15 Jorge Burga Bartra,
'Barriada y vivienda: Memoria
e identidad tipológica', lecture
at the Instituto Goethe, Lima,
Peru, 2001.
16 Lars Lerup, *Das Unfertige
Bauen (Building the
unfinished)*, Bauwelt
Fundamente, Vieweg & Sohn
(Braunschweig), 1986, p 87.
17 Susan B Lobo, *Tengo casa
propia*, IEP (Lima), 1984, p 175ff.
18 Analysed in William
Mangin, 'The role of regional
associations in the adaptation
of rural population in Peru',
Sociologus 9, Berlin 1959.
Mangin contributed the article
'The urbanization case history
(the pseudonymous
"Benavides" barriada in Lima)'
in a 1963 issue of *Architectural
Design*, and it was
subsequently published in his
seminal *Peasants in Cities,
Readings in the Anthropology*

Aspirations and Identities

The act of building is often the expression of the wish for social change.[16] No other reason makes provincial Peruvians abandon their communities and build new homes on a desert place close to the capital. Basic survival is followed by values such as progress, hard work, savings and living together, which are considered urban qualities.[17] The main aim of the settlers is to obtain the property title, which for them embodies personal fulfilment and the feeling of social acceptance.

When members of a village decide to migrate, they organise themselves in groups, mostly in a hierarchic structure, with a leader and distributed responsibilities. At the place of arrival, social networks are established and a strong relation to the abandoned community maintained. Depending on their provenance, the new settlers cope differently with the often difficult geographic and social situation and develop various economic activities to subsist. Where progress is successful, this triumph is demonstrated to the community they have come from and other *paisanos* follow.

Cultural traditions are the basis for identification and the definition of the living environment. Migrants organise themselves within regional[18] and effective voluntary associations set up without governmental support. Women run *comedores populares* (public soup-kitchens) and the Glass-of-Milk-Programme for schoolchildren as effective strategies for survival. The Andean

tradition of a shared economy is maintained and frequently produces urban self-employment.[19]

In Villa El Salvador, the creation of an industrial park was sensational and an important step towards independence and metropolitan acceptance. Shoes made in Villa are sold all over the capital, their hand-made designs inspired by European or North American prototypes copied from Internet sites. Values of modernity, such as Internet access and technical equipment, became features of the *barriadas* at the end of the 20th century. For example, public Internet *cabinas* are to be found all over the young towns, and ambitious and well-organised *barrios populares* have local radio stations and their own websites.[20]

Radical Change

The act of occupation has as wide territorial consequences for the abandoned as for the invaded landscape, and is denominated in Peru as *urbanización del campo* and *ruralización de la ciudad*. Migration has crucially changed the city scale, its social, cultural and spatial structures. *Lima Metropolitana* today covers about 800 square kilometres along the Pacific coastline.[21] The extending *mancha urbana* (urban stain) is causing the gradual disappearance of the three river valleys of Rímac, Lurín and Chillón, the erosion of the soil through the sealing of permeable surfaces, and the loss of recreation spaces. Pre-Hispanic archaeological sites and ecological resources such as the fragile microclimate of the Lomas[22] are endangered by human settlements, while economic values are the result of territorial occupation.

Right
Informal street-sellers
invading the centre of Lima.
The area around the market in
Barrios Altos in 1986. Ten
years later the area was
cleared as part of mayor
Alberto Andrade's historical
city recovery programme.

Below
The suburban landscape after
a *fiesta popular* in Villa El
Salvador.

Below
Metropolitan Institute of Planning (IMP) plan showing a proposal of the territorial organisation of greater Lima, 1992. The black and brown urbanisable areas were already urbanised by 2003.
Orange: urbanised and consolidated triangle between the historical centre of Lima, harbour city of Callao and the spas of Miraflores and Barranco
Red: urbanised areas
Black: urbanisable areas
Brown: urbanisable *barriada* areas with productive activities
Light green: untouchable natural areas
Green: protected ecological areas
Dark green: areas of recreation; reciprocal action between inner and outer city

Lima's urban spaces are fragmented and segregated. The wealthy population, living within gated communities, feels threatened by the massive extension of self-constructed areas.

contributing at least 42 per cent to the Gross National Product. A parallel informal market, described by the economist Hernando de Soto as *El otro sendero* (The other path),[23] is physically predominantly located in the old city. Suburban settlers depend on it as the main provider of cheap goods, services and work, for their clients and cheap storage room. Most migrants work in the informal sector as *ambulantes* (street sellers), offering anything imaginable on the main roads within the historic city centre, which suffers from physical deterioration. A total of 300,000 void inner-city square metres stands opposite a carpet-like extending periphery.

Lima has no underground or train system; 70 per cent of the daily suburban traffic of 170,000 buses or microbuses and 800,000 cars pass through the old city, and its public spaces are determined by the informal city around it. Since 1991, when UNESCO declared the colonial city the 'Cultural Heritage of Mankind', there has been a fight for urban space between the informal street-sellers and the authorities. Resettlement programmes in multistorey *galerías comerciales* are more or less successful, but insufficient for the growing number of *ambulantes* in an economically difficult situation.

Where Does Settlement End and City Begin?
An urban grid as such does not transform the *barriadas* into city, nor does it determine their size or guarantee their official recognition as metropolitan districts. Where is the difference between settlement and city, and where does urbanity begin? Settlement has to do with family, with community, with ethnic belonging. There is probably a common religious belief and everybody knows each other. City, in contrast, is multi-ethnic, dense and a place where multiple population groups live together in mutual exchange. Only a few *barriadas* , for example Comas, are spaces of metropolitan life where people from all over Lima gather to enjoy the new nightlife scene. But far more places have this potential.

Whether or not the *barriada* is city or the utopia of city does not depend only on the political and social processes in Peru. Whether the suburban dream dries out the inner city, or the metropolitan megalomania consumes the periphery, is also a global question. Self-organisation and participation, in terms of shared responsibility, are in fact valuable urban principles. Δ

of Urbanization (1970). Also analysed in Jürgen Golte and Norma Adams, *Los Caballos de Troya de los Invasores*, IEP (Lima), 1987.
19 Ingrid Olórtegui, 'Informal Settlers in Lima', conference at ESF/N-AERUS international workshop in Leuven and Brussels, Belgium, May 2001.
20 Comas: www.comasweb.de. Villa el Salvador: venus.inive.it/sattin/web/htm.
21 Between 1940 and 1984 the extension of Lima increased almost tenfold, from 3,900 hectares to 35,000 hectares. By 2000, a doubling, to 70,000, had taken place, and by 2015 the city is expected to cover 99,600 hectares. Source: INEI, *Tendencias del Crecimiento Urbano de Lima Metropolitana al año 2015*, INEI (Lima), 1993, p 486f.
22 The Lomas are hills where coastal fog gathers and, between July and October the desert therefore turns green.
23 Hernando de Soto, *El Otro Sendero. La Revolución Informal*, Instituto Libertad y Democracia (Lima), 1986.

Lima's urban spaces are fragmented and segregated. The wealthy population, living within gated communities, feels threatened by the massive extension of self-constructed areas. Even the officially accepted and consolidated *barriadas* suffer from their image among middle- and upper-class *Limeños* as dangerous and antisocial areas. The distribution of infrastructure, urban green, water and municipal attention to each district is closely linked with the monetary potential of its inhabitants. On the other hand, the capital has become a melting pot of all Peruvian cultures. A mixture of rural customs and global influences creates the new urban culture of the *chicha* city, which penetrates all social strata and parts of the metropolis.

Reciprocal Action Between Inner and Outer City
The *barriada* is more than suburbia; it is surrounding, conquering and overtaking the old city. The marginal city has generated an industrial and artisan development that is successful and

Dedicated to the dwellers of the Pampa de Amancaes and to the work of John FC Turner.

Kathrin Golda-Pongratz studied architecture at the TU Munich in Germany, and the ETSAB Barcelona in Spain. Her diploma project was an urban ecological intervention for Mexico City. Between 1998 and 2001 she was guest student and assistant at the Faculty of Architecture, Universidad Nacional de Ingeniería, Lima, Peru. Since 1999 she has been working on her doctoral thesis on the structural change of Lima's historic city centre, at the Institute for Urban and Regional Planning, University of Karlsruhe in Germany. She is assistant at the postgraduate architecture department of the Kunstakademie Düsseldorf, and a member of the German Association of Latin American Research (ADLAF).

Redefining

Green-ness is the obscure object of desire that has been driving the development of suburbia since its beginnings. People fled to suburbia to get away from the congested city and its dense housing blocks, polluted air and car-dominated public space. The endless plains of fields and woods became a utopian image countering the urban dystopia of continuously built fabric. But as city dwellers started to migrate into suburbia, they brought with them their civilised baggage from the city and inevitably dumped it wherever they chose to settle anew. Hence the longing image of green landscape that was the reason for most suburbanites to come here in the first place was replaced over time, the difference being that people now had no other place left to go in order to find what they were looking for.

   It is this paradox that the projects assembled here attempt to tackle. Common to all is the thesis that the degradation of landscape in suburbia is caused by

Green-ness

a constant misunderstanding, and misuse, of green space. In today's suburbia, green space is, in fact, only very rarely staged to complement the built fabric with landscape. In most cases it serves a completely different objective, namely the provision of privacy. Hence the insurpassable importance of the front garden, which is basically a set-back space texture-mapped with green lawn.

To satisfy both desires, the schemes presented here propose to deal with them separately. Privacy, on the one hand, is achieved by raising the house in the air (Greenurbia) or sinking it in the ground (Sub-'burb), which in return frees up ground space for other uses, for instance public programmes. On the other hand, landscape is maintained by programming parts of the site with non-building programmes such as parks, gardens or agricultural uses (Fischbek-Mississippi) or by introducing a strong topographical definition (Sonic Polder).

(Sonic Polder – the Su

This project, by the German architects and urban planners Bernd Kniess, is a clear demonstration of how to build on a site, just west of Cologne, that was once deemed impossible to develop due to the noise of adjacent traffic. Schirin Taraz-Breinholt describes how solving the noise problem enabled the project to exceed standard suburban residential forms by increasing spatial complexity and diversity, as well as through the incorporation of topography and infrastructure within the built fabric.

Bernd Kniess in association
with adu Cologne Institut für
Immissionsschutz, Sonic Polder,
Cologne, 2001
Design team: Bernd Kniess,
Sebastian Hauser, Leonhard
Lagos Karlhoff, Marion Mischke,
Christine Schmidt, Daniel
Schulze-Wethmar, Barbara Wolff

Right
Like the polder landscapes
along the coastlines, the site
in the city centre of Cologne
has to be reclaimed. In this
case it is threatened not by
waves of water but by sound,
from the adjacent high-speed
train and highway. This condition
becomes eponymous for the
project – Sonic Polder.

round Sound System)

When looking at a city through the eyes of the average planner, there are always a few blind spots. One of these can be found in a typical suburban neighbourhood west of Cologne, at a temptingly short distance from the city centre. To see something in such a blind spot you cannot rely on the information detected by your retina – you need more than vision. You need *a* vision, and you need brains.

Admittedly, the site is not exactly inviting. The adjacent tracks of a high-speed train in the north, a notoriously congested highway in the west, and other busy streets to the east and south make it a rather unlikely plot for a quiet residential area – despite its favourable accessibility and affluent neighbourhood. It is not the generic suburban field, lying idle for any idea to be projected onto it, but rather a site that needs to be reclaimed. Even when provided with the standard marginal noise barriers, the majority of the site would still be useless in terms of acceptable noise levels and building regulations.

The analysis of the propagation of sound waves is therefore the formative basis of the design. Rather than isolating the site with huge noise barriers at its borders, six smaller, parallel walls, traversing the site in an east–west direction, proved to be more efficient. Only after thus complying with the regulations would it be possible to start the actual construction process. By heaping the excavation from the buildings' foundations against the parallel walls, the site is transformed into an artificial protective topography. It is a very peculiar hilly landscape, designed by acoustic analysis that reclaims the site from a body of sound. But on this moulded ground the usual suburban typology (street, front garden with garage, house, rear garden) would be literally hard-pushed against the wall. The common sequence of public and semipublic zones would

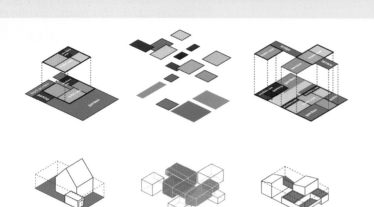

Above
The usual suburban typology is
turned inside out, its elements
redefined. Rather than pushing
the access roads to the
boundary of the plot, they are
located in the centre of the
individual plots and
incorporated in the buildings.
Main and secondary buildings
adjoin directly to the road
leaving no green space, no
deserted front garden.

Right
The differentiated public and
private spaces of the house
find their counterpart in a
wide range of green spaces
with different qualities: the
introverted patio, roof gardens
facing the street or the rear
garden, the open bridge,
crossing the access road, the
south-facing mound by the
street, or the quiet back garden.

Far right
Storyboard of the design
process: reclamation of the site
through the protective
topography, subdivision into
single plots, layout and
orientation of the buildings, and
differentiation of the different
spatial and social zones.

Below
The analysis of the propagation
of sound waves is the formative
basis of the design. Rather
than isolating the site with huge
noise barriers at its borders,
six smaller, parallel walls,
evenly distributed over the site,
proved to be more efficient.

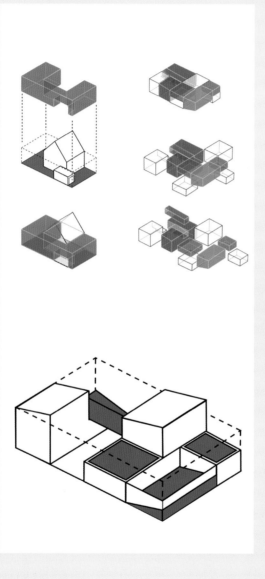

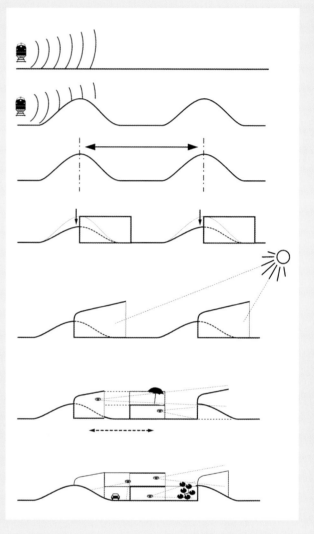

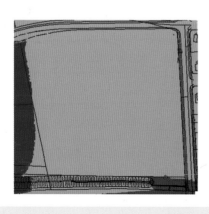

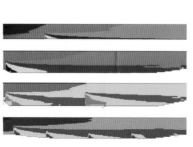

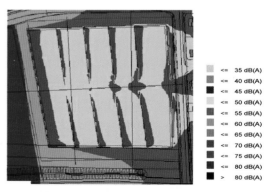

	<= 35 dB(A)
	<= 40 dB(A)
	<= 45 dB(A)
	<= 50 dB(A)
	<= 55 dB(A)
	<= 60 dB(A)
	<= 65 dB(A)
	<= 70 dB(A)
	<= 75 dB(A)
	<= 80 dB(A)
	> 80 dB(A)

Right and below
Both the main and side
building can be extended on
the second floor, the roofs of
the ground-floor volumes used
as terraces. The bridging
element can be completed as
an interior space, thus
increasing the floor space of
the building.

Bottom
Topography and typology form
an inseparable unit. The
secondary building is carved
in the mound on the smaller
strip to the north of the access
street, with ancillary functions
on the ground floor.

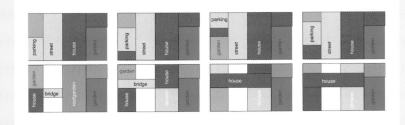

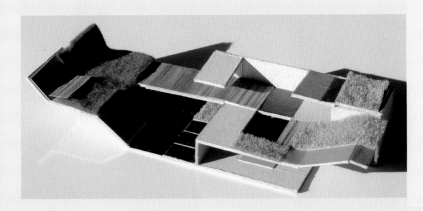

scarcely leave a wide enough strip of even ground for a house with a private back garden (which, after all, seems to be the essential constituent in the concept of suburbia). Since dumping the typical structures on the ground is no longer an option, a new typology has to be developed – one that works with the topography and treats building and landscape as one.

The access roads are located parallel to the mounds, at the base of the southern slope, thus dividing the individual plots into two parts. This seemingly counterproductive arrangement is the starting point of a strategy that turns the common suburban typology inside out. Both sides of the split plot are confined by mounds and will be used as building ground. There is no spacer, no deserted front garden; every corner of the site seems transformed into livable, inhabitable space. While the main building adjoins directly to the access road on the southern side, a secondary building is carved in the mound on the smaller strip to the north. Both can be extended and connected by a bridging element on the second floor.

All living rooms of the main house face the most secluded patio-like green space, meeting the protecting mound at the southern boundary of the plot. The defining characteristic of this space – its privacy – is maintained by the intelligent offset layout of the two-storey extensions. The whole area can therefore be declared as a patio typology, thus allowing a higher density than is usual in residential areas planned according to German building regulations.

But what is striking about Sonic Polder is not merely its economic efficiency nor its utilisation ratio. One might argue that the reclamation of a site that is currently considered inoperative is in itself quite a remarkable enhancement in value. Above all, it is the quality and differentiation of the diverse spaces that stand out. Without too much effort one can envisage a whole kaleidoscope of constellations and scenarios: young father working from home in his office on the second floor of the annex building; grandmother watching kids sledging in the protected rear garden from the living room; sleepy shift-worker enjoying the view from the quiet bedroom on the second floor; teenage daughter sunbathing on the adjacent terrace of her own little apartment, while checking out whether the neighbour's son is coming down the road; pensioner tinkering in the garage on the ground floor of the annex building; elegant hostess watching the car of arriving dinner-party guests pull up under the bridging room … The list could go on for a while without necessarily reaching the otherwise inevitable suburban scenario of 'suicidal garden gnome hiding beneath a common boxwood in tidy deserted front garden'. The complexity and diversity of the spatial vocabulary is considerable and is even increased by the different widths of the plots.

Right and bottom right
Aerial views by day and by night. Despite its strong typological guidelines, Sonic Polder is not a monotonous addition of identical elements, but a complex and diverse structure.

Below
The development scheme shows that every corner of the site is transformed into livable, inhabitable space. The whole area can be declared as a patio typology, thus allowing a higher density than is usual in residential areas planned according to German building regulations.

Opposite (top) and right
By incorporating the road in
the buildings, Sonic Polder has
the potential to develop a
community without gates. The
public space of the road
becomes more intimate,
protecting the houses from
uninvited visitors without
armed guards. Rather than
being a mere piece of
infrastructure, the road
becomes a livable space.

Below
View from the patio through
the main building into the
rear garden. The opposition
of building and garden is
dissolved.

Redefining the suburban elements in this new typology reveals the failures of the original condition. The strict separation of public and private space in suburbia, usually reinforced by defensive fortifications such as walls, hedges or fences, provokes a social structure that is based on isolation. Contact, when inevitable, is considered rather awkward and preferably reduced to a polite nod in the morning. A sense of community would probably have to be dictated by the plenary meetings of the Neighbourhood Watch, since it is clearly not encouraged through the built environment.

By incorporating the road in the buildings, Sonic Polder has the potential to develop a community without gates. The public space of the road becomes more intimate, protecting it from uninvited visitors without armed guards. Rather than being a mere piece of infrastructure, the road becomes a livable space. In turn, the private space of the house becomes, to some extent, more public without losing the possibility for retreat. The variety of plot sizes and housing types promotes a more differentiated user profile. And last but not least, the design and differentiation of green spaces finally grants them an adequate significance. It seems paradoxical how often this undeniable potential of life outside the city centre is neglected by its planners. Green space can be so much more than a spacer.

Sonic Polder can be seen as a typical project of Kniess' practice. Rather than avoiding the obstacles of a difficult site, the architects strive for the challenge of the seemingly impossible. Their material, which they handle with virtuosity, consists just as much of concrete slabs as of the usually shunned, but extensive, body of German building rules and regulations. And just like that, they overcome the restrictive architectural stereotypes that have always been taken for granted. Δ

Jones, Partners: Architecture,
Sub'burb, California, 2000
Design team: Wes Jones, Doug
Jackson, Jim Rhee, George
Telosa, Aryan Omar, Arlene Lee,
Kaoru Murayama, Dora Jones,
Jean Young

Above
With its park-like nature on
the elevated public level, the
Sub-'burb appears as a green
island/carpet in the Californian
desert, east of Los Angeles.
The exposed walls of the
outermost units mark its
present extension as a
perimeter wall, but are
reabsorbed into the fabric
as the pattern grows in the
future.

Sub-'burb

Access to outdoor space and concerns for privacy are two main issues for those living in suburbia. The suburbs of southern California are formed by ever-appreciating property prices, as plots get filled by bigger houses leaving less open space between neighbours and for the use of the inhabitants. In Sub-'burb, **Wes Jones** of Jones, Partners: Architecture shows a model that responds to economic pressure by maintaining the suburban balance between privacy and display, and to the demands of ecology and an increasing computer and cyberworld.

For better or for worse, the garden suburbs are what America came up with when presented with the chance to create its own ideal geography. A hundred years of confrontation with a vast, untamed frontier taught America the virtues of open space, while the subsequent hundred years of coping with the loss of that frontier forced lessons in getting along with the neighbours. The frontier period promoted individualism and self-reliance, and the expectation of freedom. The contemporary version of these is found in the millions of microfrontiers that make up suburbia. But what has been lost can also be laid to this new geography: the hoarding of this hard-won comfort has made the suburb the perfect embodiment of controlled individualism, and the plot the spatial equivalent of the straitened individual in a society of similar spaces. The hysterical banality and parcelled imperialism of the tracts stand neatly for the conformity and small-mindedness its inhabitants are thought to exhibit.

At its root the suburb is a compromise between a rural ideal, with its implication of individual freedom, and the economic imperative to concentrate labour and the needs for infrastructure. Seething under the clichéd, placid surface is a complex confusion of competing forces and interests – economic, social, physical – and the compromise that set this in motion haunts all aspects of the continuing suburban dynamic. This is nowhere more evident than in southern California where the suburb's usual attractions are exaggerated by a boom-town economy, laid-back lifestyle and glorious beachfront setting.

There is no natural order to the suburbs. Plot sizes and configurations were originally determined by the banks and developers according to what size mortgage they felt the average prospective home owner could support, rather than by considerations of light and air,

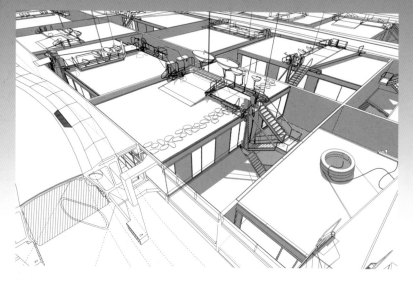

Above
From the public (roof) level, the home owner enters his or her dwelling through the courtyard at the lower (ground) level. Below the roads at the public level lies the infrastructure of the tract (energy, sewer, water, data) along with (rock-bed) thermal storage that provides naturally conditioned air.

Below
The courtyard housing units of the Sub-'burb form a continuous carpet of habitation twice as dense as the existing suburban model. Lifting the classical front lawn onto the roof (Corbu's fifth facade reaches California) allows for a direct adjacency of the houses without the usual set-backs.

Opposite, top
The courtyards provide privacy and natural lighting for the interior spaces. Equipped with plants and a pond area, they promote evaporative cooling and humidification to create a comfortable microclimate.

Opposite, bottom
The green park-like upper surface, a patchwork of lawns dotted with palms, latently evokes the garden-city ideal of early 20th-century Californian suburbs. However, the seemingly pastoral atmosphere is cross-cut by an omnipresent technology, ranging from electrically driven personal vehicles to the uncanny proliferation of satellite dishes on the roof.

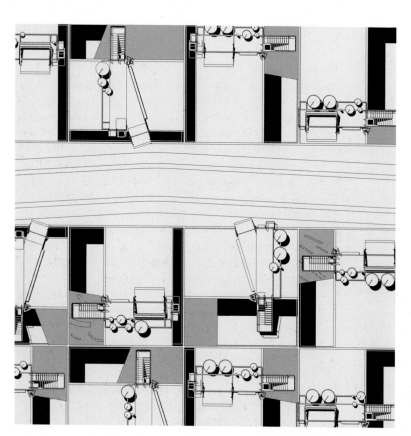

human comfort or aesthetic criteria. The road systems were laid out either in picturesque winds that implied a topography that did not exist, or in grids that ignored the topography that did. Lush greenery sprouted in ordered patches of former desert or across ancient sand dunes. The power to ignore or invent nature in this way comes from the real-estate engine, which in southern California is totally souped up.

Property always appreciates in southern California. The certainty of rising land-values creates a pressure to build that leads to revealing absurdities. In the established communities, where sprawl is not an option, the unnatural effect of increasing property values in the suburb is decreasing space: not in the sense that it becomes solely a commodity for the rich, and so less is available to pass around to everyone else, but in the more literal sense that the land appears to shrink as it becomes more expensive. This is because the economic pressures on the land do not translate into the increased population density, but into an increase in building density. There is less apparent space, and less effective space, because there is more, bigger stuff filling that space for the same number of people. The ruthless economy of speculation that has grown up to take advantage of this (un)natural law of appreciation is producing a second growth of super-sized suburban housing to replace the first utopian wave of bungalows that are now 'undervalued'.

Despite its artificial nature (in both senses) and compromised genesis, the suburb is not really a bad place to live, as more than 20 million Angelenos would attest. But what is good about it is threatened by the aggressive expansion of the physical plant. The original structures, while small, were carefully tuned to the garden-city ideal that made these tracts so attractive. Schindler, Neutra and the Case Study architects showed that the 'California dream' is lived outdoors: at the beach, or around the pool in the back yard, barbecuing, or in the driveway, shooting baskets or washing the car. The canvas-clad sleeping baskets of the King's Road house and sweeping terraces of the Lovell health house, as well as the broad picture-windows and sliding glass doors of the Case Study houses forced the occupants (for their own good) out into 'nature', known locally as the yard. The new growth of 'pocket mansions' or 'tract monsters' sacrifices even this small remnant of the garden-city ideal to maxed-out zoning envelopes that leave no space for more than notional 'yards', forcing the residents back inside to the less salubrious pleasures of their TVs.

The greatest casualty of this creeping gigantism is the paradigmatic suburban concern for privacy – forcing a more urban inwardness onto the naturally extroverted suburb. The blank urban corridor and facade of anonymous windows serve a similar purpose to the suburban set-backs, landscaping and

back-yard fence, but what 'works' in the city would be a disaster out in the suburb. And yet, the looming neighbours and reduced yard set-backs play havoc with the characteristic suburban balance, uniquely struck outdoors, between effective isolation and community display.

The fences and yards that provide isolation also become signs of that desire and, as such, engage the publicness of interpretation. The urban assurance of privacy through anonymity is counter to the suburban desire for status display. In the suburb, privacy is maintained through subordination to the spatial ordering of the tract and conformity to its 'norms'. This keeps the 'other' in line by preventing the 'other' from being unduly noticed, yet still allows the registering of status in the degree of conspicuous consumption. The pressure to build bigger makes it harder to sustain this wilful blindness, though, as the differences in degree hit the wall, other outlets to assert prestige are sought.

A result is the rise of design review boards that enforce with 'guidelines' what formerly was assured by peer pressure and spatial relief. The design review board phenomenon has grown out of the suburban obsession with property values. Where security in the city is related to personal safety, in the suburbs it means protection of stuff. Yet, the stuff must be on view, not hidden away. In the suburb, stuff is secure if it's on the lawn, in the driveway – beyond that all-powerful but invisible property line. The main thing on display is that property, though – the trophy lawn, the heroic driveway, not to mention the Mediterranean/Tudor/French provincial/ranch castle overlooking these – and the security of this is achieved by embedding it within a robust system of value that makes these invisible boundaries have meaning. This meaning is itself derived from a respect for the possibility of individual dominion over a piece of land, and is established in the ability to walk around one's house. And this is generally felt to be the essence of the suburb. As the land shrinks, this essence evaporates.

The suburb is likely to continue to evolve under the pressure of the impossible economics, and the influence of the cyber and green revolutions will also soon be felt. The computer revolution will promote an empowering decentralisation, while green-ness will encourage a contrasting population densification. These opposed tendencies will be magnified by the economic imperatives of the real-estate dynamic as they are played out within the context of the American dream and its California suburban version. Ironically, given their reputation, the suburbs are both the test market and final resting place of architectural innovation. The complacent success of the 'burbs makes them resistant to change, but also makes them places where change finally becomes ratified after it has proven itself elsewhere.

The suburbs have been classically decentralised, but in a way that assumed the sanctity and primacy of the nuclear family unit – which has lately fissioned. The family is evolving into a mini society: the individual members, at all ages, are becoming more independent, economically and socially, and in the best cases are given greater freedom and responsibility for the definition of the family realm. Popular journalism has decried this as a negative result of an outwardly fragmented society and the loss of family values, but it is equally possible to explain it as a result of technology like the mobile phone and credit card that provides security and power to even the youngest family members. This fragmentation has been reflected in the increase in the typical number of bedrooms and other spaces where family members can get away from each other. The real-estate industry has seen this as an opportunity to proliferate ameliorative features and compensatory spaces that can be listed as amenities to drive up the price of the family house.

The suburbs have been classically decentralised, but in a way that assumed the sanctity and primacy of the nuclear family unit – which has lately fissioned. The family is evolving into a mini society: the individual members, at all ages, are becoming more independent, economically and socially, and in the best cases are given greater freedom and responsibility for the definition of the family realm.

Above
The mobile program deck, a patented activity-support and space-definition system, provides the programme of a typical three-bedroom suburban house in less than half the space.

Right
Access to the home is provided by a mobile staircase that appears as a domesticated version of the Venice Beach outdoor fitness studio. By pedalling this structure from one end of the plot to the other, the home owner can also mow the lawn, mulch the trimmings or charge the household's batteries.

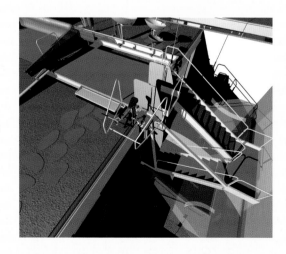

This fragmentation has been pushed along by the advent of the Internet, which encourages the individual escape into cyberspace. While it is probably too much to claim that the public space of the future will be electronic and, thus, that physical public-gathering space will no longer be necessary, it is true that this cyber realm will offer relief both for the individual from the family and for the family itself from the neighbours. This means that cyberspace will supplement the yard space in a sense, and that telecommuting will allow the worker to be located anywhere he or she wishes – out of the city or in the bedroom.

The suburbs have been classically green, but paradoxically at a cost to the environment; to achieve their condition of artificial lushness they have sprawled over otherwise unspoiled territory, paving over the native soil or redefining it with the wonders of plant foods and weedkillers. Like a golf course, which idealises the natural but purifies it to an abstraction that bears little resemblance to its model, the garden-city suburb draws borders around its graded nature: fairways and rough, traffic islands and front lawns.

These are the issues that the present scheme for a new model suburb addresses. This 'Sub-'burb' responds to the economic pressures on the limited landscape to increase density, and to the related need to maintain the unique suburban balance between privacy and display despite such density; it answers the necessity for greater ecological responsibility and takes account of the reorientation towards spatial reality prompted by the increasing importance of the computer and cyberworld.

The Sub-'burb proposes a continuous carpet of habitation that is approximately twice as dense as the existing suburban model, but which confines all the building below the circulation datum so that the park-like nature of the garden-city ideal is emphasised at the public level. The openness of this field of lawns is preserved through the use of air-bag guardrails, which provide fall protection only when needed. The status-display function of suburbia is satisfied at the upper, public level, without bulking up the house, by separating the functions of dwelling and storage; since all the courtyard houses are out of sight, status is conveyed by the quality of stuff rather than the size of the house, and these possessions – cars, satellite data services, meal services – are arranged on a mobile platform for the neighbour's inspection.

The infrastructure for the tract lies in the space below the roads, and includes energy,

This fragmentation has been pushed along by the advent of the Internet, which encourages the individual escape into cyberspace. While it is probably too much to claim that the public space of the future will be electronic and, thus, that physical public-gathering space will no longer be necessary, it is true that this cyber realm will offer relief both for the individual from the family and for the family itself from the neighbours.

sewer, water and data, along with access tunnels. Also located under the roadbed proper is a rock-bed thermal storage area that supplies ceiling and floor plenums in the adjacent houses with conditioned air, heated or cooled according to the season. The increased density allows for the provision of a neighbourhood-sized strip of open space at the public level for each group of 40 houses.

Below the public level, the courtyard for each residence provides complete privacy, efficiently accessing just the right amount of outdoors and nature necessary to promote a sense of well-being without intruding into the neighbour's perceptual field or sprawling beyond its needs. Each courtyard is designed to provide for microclimate adjustment, using a balance of plantings and a pond area to promote the evaporative cooling and humidification so crucial to comfort in a desert setting.

Access to each house is through this courtyard, entered from above by a stair and lift device appended to the mobile display platform. This device can be pedalled from one end of the plot to the other, providing the resident with exercise as well as mowing the lawn, mulching the trimmings, and supplying additional power to the household batteries. Inside, the house is organised to provide all the programme of a typical three-bedroom suburban house in less than half the space, through the use of a mobile program deck (MPD). The area of the house is divided in half longitudinally, into zones of greater or lesser programmatic control; one half is taken up by the shuttling pods of the program deck while the other half is left open as free space. The MPD takes advantage of the fact that in the typical dwelling only a few of the rooms are ever being used simultaneously, and eliminates the space of the unused rooms, or rather trades it for additional unprogrammed free space. This additional area serves as the family's political space, where the individual members must negotiate its disposition at any particular time. ⚏

Greenurbia, Or the Return of the Wolves

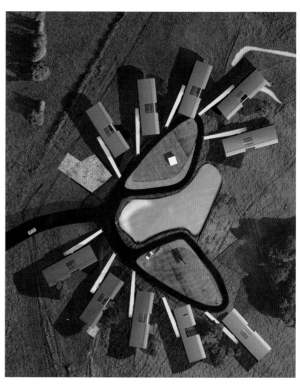

The forerunner of today's suburbia, the 19th-century garden-city movement, was posed as a solution to the impaired quality of life in industrialised cities. Suburbia itself is now coming under scrutiny, as its serious impact on nature and the environment is questioned. **J Pablo Molestina** of Gruppe MDK asks how ecological concerns might be introduced into suburbia. With Greenurbia he proposes a light suburbanism for the German Ruhr, where the ground remains untouched as much as possible, allowing for the establishment of self-regulating ecosystems.

J Pablo Molestina of Gruppe
MDK with William Lyons Jr,
Greenurbia, German Ruhr,
2002
Construction: Roland Schmitz

Opposite
Individual houses gather
around an 'urban pod'.
At the centre, the pond for
rain-/brown-water processing,
to its sides, two playing fields,
each grouping up to seven
houses. Around the fields
winds a narrow paved strip
for access, which collects the
visitor parking spaces. The
local power plant is beneath
the upper field.

Above
A young cluster set in the
fields and seen from afar. In
time, the fields will turn into
forest, and the houses will
recede into the green.

Suburban houses are familiar. They have a lawn
that is green and a driveway. Maybe a modest
front porch. In the back yard there is a patio or
deck, and perhaps a barbecue grill as well.
Neighbours are on the other side of the fence. We
know their names. On the street, children play.

The persistence of this benevolent cultural
cliché is not to be underestimated. Even while
the European megalopolises around the Ruhr
and elsewhere in Europe shrink in population,
their absolute size, the total 'urbanised' surface,
is growing due to the unbroken expansion of
suburban housing. This is due to the demands
increasing expectations of space per dweller,
and also to the increasing number of small and
single households. But most importantly, it is
due to people still moving away from traditional
urban apartment-dwelling in search of a
different lifestyle associated with living in a
freestanding house set in 'green'.

The expectation is that life in the suburbs will
be more private and more tied to the outdoors,
that the experience of nature in one's own
garden and in public green spaces will become
intrinsic to everyday life. The reality is, however,
that to satisfy the demand for a suburban
lifestyle, large expanses of landscape are used
up. Streets are laid out over the land; extensive
networks for sewage, water, heating and
electricity are built underground, stretched to
the limits and often hovering at the edge of
breakdown. Houses are then set in a 'landscape
platter' with a symbolic front garden of close
to no ecological value. Paved and built surfaces
often cover over 70 per cent of the total plot
area, this not including streets and paved
infrastructure. The geometry of suburban

settlements, with their fences and territorial
delineations, is more prone to reveal the wealth of its
residents than to offer a habitat for wildlife and plants
– the basic features of landscape quality.

Given this suburban house model, the very desire
to drive out of the city and to live in a 'landscaped'
suburban setting subverts the qualities of the
landscape, creating vast suburban areas that are an
ecological burden, themselves the greatest impediment
to the establishment of natural ecosystems. The notion
of nature as embodied in the suburbs today is a
hopelessly formal one. While it provides the appearance
of 'green', its physical features actually exclude most
forms of animal and plant life. It is a 'green' realm
where people may allow some planting to settle, but it
is not a form of landscape where people and animals,
'cultural plants' and wildlife, can coexist.

And yet our visceral understanding of what the
'natural setting' is has shifted away from typical park-like
visions of nature that were prevalent in the European
tradition and were given physical expression in the great
American parks of Frederick Law Olmsted and the like.
The assumption was that human intelligence, through a
relentless blueprint, could organise and form all features
of the natural. Our new perception of the natural is less
naive, more planetary, not driven by human-comfort
needs but more open to, and accepting of, the power of
the wilderness.

This is the vision of nature that we encounter in the
poetry of Pablo Neruda and in the vast landscapes of
his native Chile. We know today that the complexity of
natural processes that we have long sought to control
and form is such that we cannot succeed in harnessing
them, for there is probably no greater power than the
self-regulating energy of the landscape. We know the
physical world regulates itself ultimately, that there is
no ecological outrage (suburban green lawns in the

Cultural consciousness and political demand for the recovery of landscape values, including native flora and fauna, is fortunately at a historical high point today. Both the personal lifestyle demand for living in the suburbs, as well as the real need for restructuring large surfaces of obsolete heavy-industry production, such as those in the German Ruhr, result in great interest in models for green architecture and planning.

desert, CO_2 emissions) without ecological catastrophe (the drying up of large natural lakes, earth warming), and yet we cling to the notion of the thoroughly planned, the foreseeable. Our planning practices are designed for total control. Our knowledge of natural processes, however, shows that there is a doomed naivety in this.

Cultural consciousness and political demand for the recovery of landscape values, including native flora and fauna, is fortunately at a historical high point today. Both the personal lifestyle demand for living in the suburbs, as well as the real need for restructuring large surfaces of obsolete heavy-industry production, such as those in the German Ruhr, result in great interest in models for green architecture and planning. Central Europeans generally seem to want to develop recovery strategies for large expanses of territory, but the market lacks models for implementing this in the context of unbridled suburban-house expansion.

Yet if the energy going into suburban-house construction were to be imbued with a strategy for re-greening the territory, allowing plants and wildlife to resettle in suburbia, we might consider the present situation a big opportunity, where both cultural awareness and market dynamics might cooperate to generate a new suburban landscape. A new form of suburban settlement would have to satisfy market demand through an integration of the artificial (our houses and the outdoor spaces we use) into a territorial pattern that leaves enough open, unplanned space to allow the 'natural' to unfold by itself. In an iterative process, the landscape should be able to regenerate itself around houses. Local forms of plants and trees could settle and even the bison and the wolf, which once populated the European plains, could return.

Past experience shows that the amount of investment undertaken in the forced 'renaturalisation' of territory often has little effect on the speed of its 'recovery'. It appears that a strategy that 'frees' areas of territory to become 'wild' and to transform themselves at their own pace, results most quickly in sustainable ecosystems of ever-growing complexity, and most directly begins to display the sort of complex self-regulating biotic processes that we associate with landscape. Even in areas where heavy industry has left great residual toxicity in the ground, it is today thought better to 'pack in' the toxic volume (so as to impede seepage into the surrounds) and to include it, like a large, inert rock, in a self-regulating expanse of wilderness.

At the end of the 19th century, the garden-city movement proposed settlement models where the continuity of green spaces was seen as a means of providing relief to the overpopulated cities and preventing mass urban immigration. A real understanding of ecology was lacking. The property patterns of the typical garden city created a structure of extensively used, fenced-in, isolated private territories, where natural continuity of space – the basic

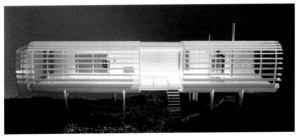

requirement for the development of flora and
fauna – was missing. The landscape around the
houses in the garden city was effectively broken
down into small gardens or lawns for private use
which, though of recreational value, were mostly
addressing a symbolic need: they were the
moated turf on which every man's castle was set.

The garden-city movement, arguably the
root of many of today's suburban formal
developments, was a cultural and political
manifesto more bent upon questioning the
quality of life in European cities at the time than
concerned with preserving or developing any
real ecological qualities of landscape, such as
biotic activity or diversity of animal and plant
species. Unfortunately, the formal model of the
garden-city housing settlement, with its curving
streets suggesting a nonexisting topography
and its hierarchical division of open space into
small-private and large-open, remains the
formal paradigm of suburban planning today.
The model is no longer adequate. Any new
attempt to deal seriously with issues of
landscape quality in the context of suburban
living has to allow the natural realm to control
large surfaces of territory.

The Greenurbia house project may be
understood at two levels: as a proposal for a
form of settlement, with implications for the
infrastructure and large-scale qualities of an
area, and also as a proposal for a kind of
suburban house product on its own piece of
land. Since suburban spatial quality by definition
results from the aggregation of many small-
scale interventions within a larger infrastructure
framework, it is clear that any territorial
proposals need to grow out of the small-scale,

but that their quality for landscape regeneration can
be tested only at the large-scale level.

The Level of the Settlement

The Greenurbia project is based on the following three
settlement principles.

Continuity of Natural Space

The best strategy for the renaturalisation of large areas
of territory is to let nature use its own evolutionary
process to recreate ecological systems of high
sustainability at a large scale. Since the natural
process of the building of ecosystems is a very complex
iterative process, which is difficult to emulate, a
strategy of 'non-intervention' in the restructuring of
the territory is the most appropriate. The scale of the
areas to be renaturalised is important: the larger the
scale, the more likely it is that plant and animal life
will gradually settle back in. We do not need to model
natural processes. We just need to create conditions
to let them happen.

Partial-Intensive Use of Open Space

Our understanding of 'living in green' must change from
one that eats up large amounts of space and turns it
into visual suburban images of green regardless of
local conditions, into one that respects the inaccessible
'otherness' of nature and, yet, intelligently settles
islands of intensive use within this natural habitat. The
strategy must turn from being one of low or occasional
use of large expanses of territory (extensive use, classic
suburbia), to one that allows a high or intensive use
of small expanses of territory. This is the difference
between the current typical suburban land-use pattern
and the land-use pattern we see in, say, mobile-home
parks. The 'extensive' land-use strategy of suburbia
covers the landscape and transforms it into a large

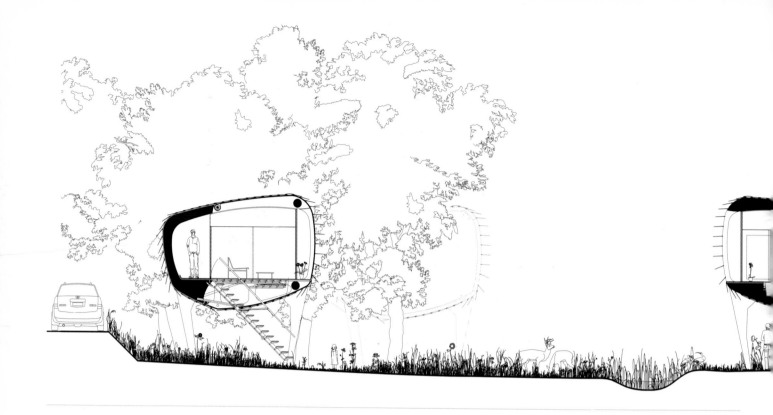

aggregation of small private plots of little-used outside spaces, foreign to local climatic and natural conditions to boot. A mobile-home park, by contrast, 'preserves' the local landscape qualities and contains the individual and collectively used surfaces as much as possible. The green expanse around a trailer park retains its openness at a large scale, for herein lies the recreational quality sought by visitors. Animals and plants are sovereign within this realm; human access and use are limited outside of the intensively used core area.

If we think of the open green expanse as a green sea, then humans populate intensively used islands within this green. Private yards can be small in size but visually and ecologically 'embedded' in the green continuum. Recreational areas, such as playing fields, collective areas for users of different ages, play areas and the like, also occur as 'islands' of varying size in the green.

Decentralised Infrastructure and Services: Urban 'Pods'

Street access and parking possibilities create a common area to which all houses are tied. This area can be thought of as an 'urban pod', which includes collective technical spaces as well as social and recreational space. Just as the spatial structure of Greenurbia creates 'islands of intensive use', the technical infrastructure displays a similar attitude. Each urban pod addresses the neighbourhood's need for energy, water, streets and all other technical facilities. Brownwater and rainwater are collected and broken down on the site, partially reused for internal consumption by the houses, partially held in the form of a communal pond at the heart

of the cluster. There is a small local power plant run on biofuel to provide heat and electricity to the houses. Excess energy is pumped back into the general net.

A settlement cluster replaces the suburban street; it is an architectural entity as well as a territorial one. Next to the urban pod, the dweller is caretaker for a piece of land, but does not own it.

The Level of the House

Our housing design is based on a single-family house with two to three bedrooms on slightly under 100 square metres. The house sits on its own plot, claiming about one-eighth of an acre of land. Of this, part is for the exclusive use of the house dweller, and part is integrated into the overall urban pod. In designing the actual house, we looked for 'green' features whilst exploring criteria for 'livability' and 'buildability'. We came to the following design goals.

Free Up the Ground Plane: Elevate the Mass to Free Up the Floor

In order to maintain the green continuum and to reduce spatial displacement of the natural level, we elevate the architectural mass above the forest floor. Through a considered application of materials, we seek to create architecture through and around which air, water and light (necessities of biotic function) may reach the ground below.

Let Water Reach the Ground Plane

One of the prevalent reasons for the ecological failure of the raised houses of modern architecture lies in their section. If we want some biotic activity to take place underneath the mass of a building, it is essential to bring light and water to this 'underneath'. A rectangular house section keeps water at the perimeter of the house, and creates a dry, shadowed area underneath

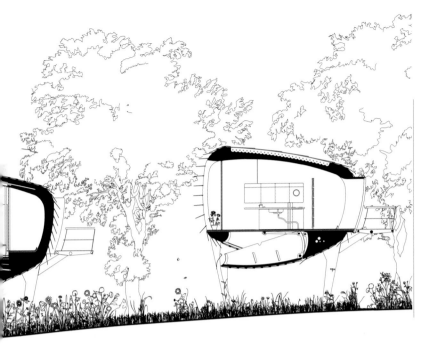

that cannot function biologically. A house high above the ground allows, by itself, a good lighting underneath it. If, in addition, the house has a rounded belly, water will be led around and underneath this volume and will reach the ground below.

No Basement or Attic
The combination of a rounded exterior and horizontal floor creates a series of leftover spaces in the section of the house, which are usable as storage areas in the kitchen floor, or technical areas for local water boilers and transformers and relay stations. Similarly, seldom-used goods can be stowed away here. The traditional basement is redundant. Areas for the storage and support of car spaces become subsumed within this leftover section area.

Light the Ground Plane with a Reflective Outer Skin
The outer skin is light, reflecting, fireproof and strong. The world of porcelain provided for our study possibilities for exterior shingles of stunning translucency and hardiness. A porcelain skin, made of square shingles 35 centimetres in plan, sheathes our prototype. On the south side, the sheathing opens into a louvre surface.

Tread Lightly
The house sits on several leg pods with a hydraulic device that allows the length of the legs to adjust to season-related changes in the floor height. There are no deep foundations, merely plates for the distribution of weight on the ground. It is thus possible to constantly adjust the house to changing site conditions.

It is even conceivable to actually move the house by means of a transporter.

Industrial Production for Economy and Flexibility
The house is made up of industrialised segments, which may be combined in different ways and altered, increased or decreased to accommodate individuality and changing needs. An aluminium rib-construction like that of an aircraft is the basic repetitive module. There are modules for bathrooms, kitchens, courtyard and living spaces. The walls are made of translucent plastic air capsules to provide insulation. The interior is humidity-proof translucent plastic, with integrated fluorescent lighting rods.

Preserve the Site Qualities
Most of the damage caused by single-family houses to their environment occurs at the beginning of the construction process. When the plot turns into a building site during construction, it changes its natural features to fit the needs of an industrial production process. By choosing a factory-produced, unitary method of building requiring minimal on-site construction, the site's natural qualities are largely preserved; the building is brought onto the site preassembled, and placed on its own series of structural legs.

Only through changed forms of implementation of the suburban dream can we preserve the promise of 'living in one's own house in green'. We need to achieve a renaturalisation of the suburban landscape so that the qualities of 'site' may be delivered by 'landscape' features: a brook, a valley, the types of vegetation, the animals, insects and flowers of a 'region'. For their sake, the suburban house recedes into the background and becomes just another element integrated into the surrounding ecosystem. ▵

New From Suburbia: Agro City

Does suburbia, by its very definition, have to colonise and destroy the existing landscape? Or can one envisage a symbiosis where suburbia and the natural ecology mutually profit from one another? In their Fischbek-Mississippi project for a new expansion area of Hamburg, cet-0 and Kunst+Herbert propose the naturalist alternative. **Nancy Couling** and **Klaus Overmeyer, of cet-0,** here describe their unique development concept which combines suburban housing and farming, creating a new form of community where periphery dwellers become rangers, and public parks a productive landscape.

cet-0 and Kunst+Herbert,
Fischbek-Mississippi,
Neugraben-Fischbek,
Hamburg, 2002
Design team: (cet-0) Klaus
Overmeyer, Nancy Couling with
Melanie Humann, Sebastian
Holtmann, Jan Kanngießer ;
(Kunst+Herbert) Bettina Kunst,
Christian Herbert with Tim Ort

Above
The common area as an extended
front garden. The scale of the
open space in the Mississippi
concept offers residents more
imaginative scope than a private
garden while, unlike with a public
park, they still enjoy the privileges
of individually determined use.

Right
'Mississippi, that's me.' An
advertising campaign advertises
the new housing development.

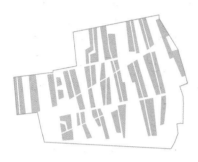

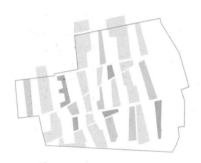

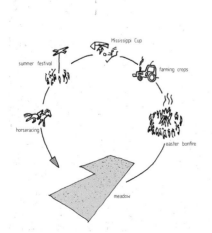

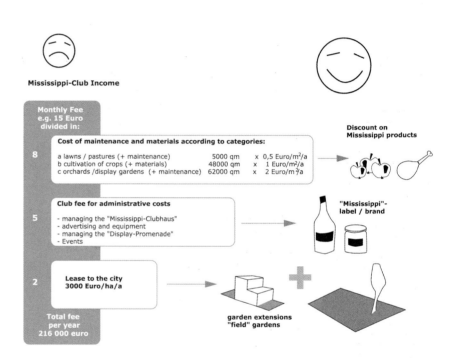

Mississippi-Club Income

	Monthly Fee e.g. 15 Euro divided in:				
8	**Cost of maintenance and materials according to categories:**				Discount on Mississippi products
	a lawns / pastures (+ maintenance)	5000 qm	x	0,5 Euro/m²/a	
	b cultivation of crops (+ materials)	48000 qm	x	1 Euro/m²/a	
	c orchards /display gardens (+ maintenance)	62000 qm	x	2 Euro/m²/a	
5	**Club fee for administrative costs**				"Mississippi"-label / brand
	- managing the "Mississippi-Clubhaus"				
	- advertising and equipment				
	- managing the "Display-Promenade"				
	- Events				
2	**Lease to the city 3000 Euro/ha/a**				garden extensions "field" gardens
	Total fee per year 216 000 euro				

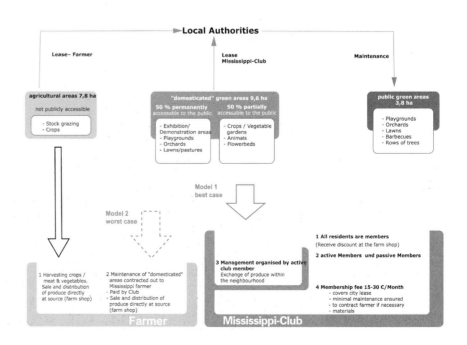

Local Authorities

Lease– Farmer · Lease Mississippi-Club · Maintenance

agricultural areas 7,8 ha
not publicly accessible
- Stock grazing
- Crops

"domesticated" green areas 9,6 ha
50 % permanently accessible to the public
- Exhibition/ Demonstration areas
- Playgrounds
- Orchards
- Lawns/pastures

50 % partially accessible to the public
- Crops / Vegetable gardens
- Animals
- Flowerbeds

public green areas 3,8 ha
- Playgrounds
- Orchards
- Lawns
- Barbecues
- Rows of trees

Model 1 best case

Model 2 worst case

1 Harvesting crops / meat & vegetables. Sale and distribution of produce directly at source (farm shop)

2 Maintenance of "domesticated" areas contracted out to Mississippi farmer
- Paid by Club
- Sale and distribution of produce directly at source (farm shop)

Farmer

3 Management organised by active club member
Exchange of produce within the neighbourhood

1 All residents are members (Receive discount at the farm shop)

2 active Members and passive Members

4 Membership fee 15-30 €/Month
- covers city lease
- minimal maintenance ensured
- to contract farmer if necessary
- materials

Mississippi-Club

The dream of home ownership, complete with hobby room, garden and garage, remains intact. Even in regions suffering from shrinking populations, the constant process of suburbanisation continues, resulting in conglomerations of single-family and terrace housing that form the amorphous periphery. Despite the abundance of inner-city sites with potential for development, most local authorities give in to the pressure to make 'greenfield' sites available. This conflict is particularly evident in Hamburg, a city marketing itself as a 'growing metropolis' in a bid to attract new residents.

Last year the city issued a three-phase cooperative design competition for a new housing area containing a total of 1,200 residential units on a site directly adjacent to the historically agricultural area of Altes Land in the outlying suburb of Neugraben-Fischbek. Runners-up Berlin-based cet-0 and Kunst+Herbert of Hamburg proposed a development concept for the area in which land for agriculture and land for building are integrally linked.

The new development will cut into, and confront, the existing landscape, and therefore, in order to give prospective inhabitants the impression of natural surroundings, the participating teams were asked to integrate connecting neighbourhood parks within their proposals. This meant looking for new models and interpretations of urban expansion into an agricultural landscape.

Can landscape be colonised yet still survive as landscape? Can a particular urbanity be defined by its agricultural character rather than its cityscape? Can periphery dwellers be more than commuters? And can they actively shape their landscape?

Our concept for Fischbek-Mississippi is based on the symbiosis of land for farming and land for building. Agricultural fields and building sites are interlocked in an alternating system of farmland, buildable plots and 'domesticated' plots, controlled and maintained by the residents. In this way, the landscape characteristic of the south Elbe region is protected, not as a preserved park but as a living entity and as an integral part of the development concept. The city authorities retain ownership of a large proportion of the green areas, however the expensive maintenance of public parks is kept to a minimum. Green areas are a combination of agricultural fields and domesticated plots, leased to an ecofarmer, or to the Mississippi Club, of which the new residents would ideally be members. Maintenance typical of urban parks is eliminated and at the same time the green areas are kept alive physically, socially and culturally through cultivation by the residents.

Mississippi – which for German speakers, due to Mark Twain's Huckleberry Finn stories, is generally associated with adventure, undisturbed nature and individual survival strategies – is the specific 'label' for this development, clearly differentiated from other residential marketing concepts. Instead of the classic and overused labels for suburban developments, such as 'park' and 'garden', or style references such as 'Spanish colonial' and 'Tuscany', borrowed from American New Urbanism, the label Fischbek-Mississippi transmits its own lifestyle, over and above the urban structure and architectural form. The label is also the programme, where the dialogue between ecological farming and the living areas generates a new form of participation, and where the residents are involved in establishing and physically forming their own environment. For example, residents are able to keep ponies, bees, tend a large vegetable garden, plant fruit trees, exercise or mow lawns. The resulting, enthusiastically produced, products such as honey,

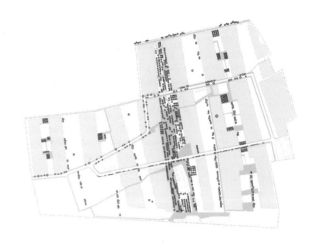

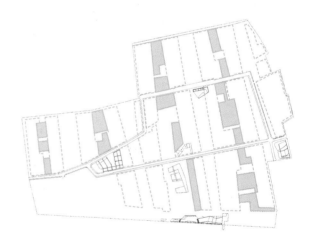

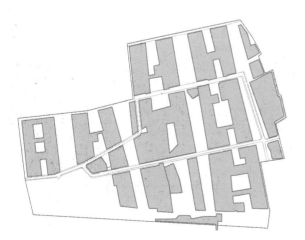

Strip C
Scattered orchard strip: facilities such as small playing fields, lawns, hedged cabinets and perennial gardens are embedded in the strip.

Strip A
a mosaic of small plots with high-density mixed use such as gardens, lawns, pony-runs, soccerfields, a lawnmowing club, active playgrounds, and barbecue areas.

Strip E
A patchwork of fields, similar to Strip A.

Strip D
Agricultural fields: gardens, strawberry fields, flowers, or gardens leased and tended by the farmer in which small grassed and play-areas are integrated.

Strip B
Mississippi shop-window: central promenade from the train station to the clubhouse, flanked with display gardens, juice production, community services, markets and a fruit-tree nursery.

marmalade and fruit juice, would be sold and marketed in the Mississippi Clubhouse, Mississippi-lifestyle included.

Due to the multiple and changing use, domesticated plots become a dynamic natural environment. As members of the Mississippi Club, residents decide annually how the communal fields will be used and/or planted. Depending on interest and commitment, the plots are either intensively planned or, in the worst-case scenario, administered by the ecofarmer with minimal vegetation. The club is obliged to keep 50 per cent of these areas accessible to the public.

In addition to the 'hard' rules – the instruments necessary to compile a planning document in urban design, such as fixing maximum density and building typologies – realisation of the Mississippi concept is also dependent on additional 'soft' rules, particularly in the initial phases of development. The Mississippi pioneers are part of the decision-making process right from the beginning. Soft rules are applied in the organisation of particular activities and events for the residents, for example small festivals, horse races, guided walks, or setting up the farm shop for local produce, and an outdoor kindergarten.

The Mississippi scout, based in the clubhouse, not only markets plots and advises potential buyers, but also encourages them to lease part of the communal garden, to use the pony pen or to form a building group with other residents. In this way small groups of friends with similar ideas can determine the built arrangement of their sites. Residents identify themselves with their larger neighbourhood unit, established and developed by two housing groups sharing a communal garden.

Compared to the conventional housing development, Agro City boasts great advantages for its residents. Through the integration of a productive and continuously utilisable 'landscape' into the built fabric, a wide range of unconventional activities becomes available for children and adults alike, as well as encouraging an awareness of seasonal changes and food-chain links in the natural environment. The scale of the open space in the Mississippi concept offers residents more imaginative scope than a private garden while, unlike with a public park, they still enjoy the privileges of individually determined use. This model is also to the advantage of the local authorities, who are freed from the responsibility and the cost of maintaining public parks. At the same time, in the place of such parks, the public space contains distinct new qualities.

The Fischbek-Mississippi concept does not claim to be a patented recipe for solving the complex relationships between city and landscape. Hamburg also lacks the courage to realise the project on such a large scale. Nonetheless, it would be worthwhile for many peripheral urban areas to experiment with these concepts and take a step towards changing the dynamics of the suburbanisation process. Mississippi is still looking for the right laboratory. Ð

Opposite, left
Top to bottom: Circulation, drainage system, public space.

Opposite, right
Top to bottom: Vegetation plan, public infrastructure, use of public space.

Below
The public space contains distinct new qualities. Through the integration of a productive and continuously utilisable 'landscape' into the built fabric, a wide range of unconventional activities becomes available.

Image of

Why is it that urban design has so little impact on suburbia? The answer is, because urbanists keep on colonising it with a concept of space that is inextricably linked with the urban matter of the city. It's the notion of a negative space moulded by the positive space of buildings that frame it, and this gives rise to urban typologies such as square, street or courtyard. In suburbia, this dialectical relationship between full and void does not exist, as its built fabric presents itself as a mass of singular spots loosely scattered across the surface of the landscape. Density is replaced by distance. Yet the distance needs to be bridged if space is to keep its operativity.

This is achieved by an excess of (auto)mobility for one part, and a forest of traffic signage to make hidden spatial relationships visible. In the classical city, this function was served by prominent buildings. Set as highly visible landmarks at strategic positions in the city, they organised the perceptual field and steered flows of movement

Suburbia

through urban space. If architecture wants to exert this role in suburbia as well, it has to attain a spatial presence that works with the scale and extension of suburban space.

Common to the projects introduced in this section is the attempt to imbue architecture with iconic elements that act as a kind of pictorial signage to navigate space. Lyons Architects imprints a building with a scaled representation of another standing next to it in such a way as to visually enlarge the distance between them – a *mise-en-scène* that is revealed to the viewer only through his or her actual movement from A to B. Likewise, in Zaha Hadid's Terminus Hoenheim-Nord, the asphalt of the car park features a giant concrete figure whose contours can be perceived only when 'scanning' it from the car or on foot. And Belgium architects 51N4E picture the suburban residential streetscape by articulating it as an athletics track that combines the qualities of both image and infrastructure.

Athletic Atmosphere

Through the recovering of neglected public space, 51N4E Space Producers introduce an innovative typological shift for a suburb development in Flanders. A scaled athletics track serving as an access road provides a new kind of suburban public space that imbues the area with a much-needed identity. **Ilka and Andreas Ruby** explore the effects of the intervention on its context, as it turns the relationship between figure and ground upside down.

The client's brief for the Flanders project called for a community centre and the development of a private housing typology for 35 houses. Rather than focusing on the design of 35 private typologies – which seemed redundant given the bland context – 51N4E proposed a powerful infrastructural approach, deliberately aiming at a contextual angle. The existing sports centre and adjacent soccer field were the trigger that gave the project its momentum. The injected infrastructure – a scaled athletics track – complements the existing sports context and imbues the newly planned allotment with a daring instant identity.

The track provides a clear-cut unity, which virtually any kind of architecture, programme or shape can plug into. Each resident can reach for his or her private sky. This short track connects the street to the soccer field. In this way a condensed avenue emerges, along which the existing sports centre is sided by the new open-air community centre, with its stands overlooking the housing infrastructure.

Thus the Allotment Athletica project seems to turn the hierarchies of the brief upside down. Instead of dealing with the figure of suburbia (the private dwellings) it prefers to work on its ground (the hitherto neglected public space) which is reinterpreted as an athletics track. Yet if the chronological order of the process is analysed, the relationship between figure and ground is again reversed: as the actual intervention, it is the track that appears as the actual figure and the dwellings as its contextual ground. This surprising emergence of sports in the middle of an ordinary residential environment could be seen in parallel with the ready-made principle; that crucial dispositive through which, early in the 20th century, Marcel Duchamp questioned the authority of a museum to decide what is art and what is not – for example by introducing a urinal into the sacred halls of art, as in his famous work 'Fountain', of 1911.

If we transfer this logic of 'object-import' to the 51N4E project, then the track reads as if it is introduced into the suburb as an object. However, upon closer inspection the analogy falls short because the transfer between object and context takes place in the opposite direction: while the museum with its institutional aura elevates the urinal to a work of art, the athletics track transforms its surroundings with its idiosyncratic atmosphere. It acts as an identity provider and enables the suburb to distinguish itself from countless others, which to all intents and purposes look exactly the same. In Duchamp's case, however, the museum still presents the dominant identity of the situation (after all, one does not have the feeling of being in the men's room). In 'Fountain', it is ultimately only the nature of the object that changes (the everyday object becoming a work of art). In 'Allotment Athletica', on the other hand, the athletics track interferes so much with the suburban

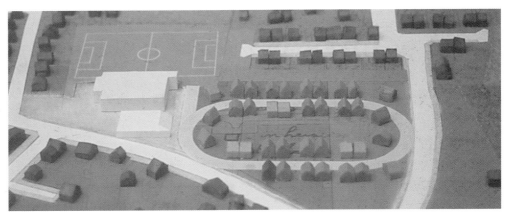

streetscape that the character of the context as a whole is changing.

The reason for this change is not some kind of cross-programming à la Tschumi, even if it seems to be indirectly inspired by it. For it is not so much the programme but the atmosphere of a programme (athletics) that produces a friction with the space (the suburban street) into which it is introduced. However, the incompatibility of action (sports) and space (suburban street) remains implicit; it is not spelt out. Its actual mission is to strip the space of the behavioural codes that are imprinted on it by its programme in order to allow different kinds of behaviour to unfold in that space. These new behavioural patterns are introduced in an evocative manner, similar to how, in a film, the insertion of a contrasting soundtrack may completely change the meaning of an image.

This process is radically different from the ready-made. The intervention affects its context so deeply that it no longer manifests itself as an isolated object but is swallowed up in the changing of the entire situation. Marcel Broodthaers presented this principle as a paradigm in his 'Jardin d'Hiver', installed in the Palais de Beaux Arts in Brussels in 1974. The installation consisted of an unusual combination of pictures and objects. The pictures showed representations that seemed to have been taken from zoological and botanic encyclopedias of the 19th century. They were shown either in picture frames hung on the wall or horizontally displayed in old-fashioned wooden display cases as one knows them from natural history museums. In addition, however (and this played a decisive role), Broodthaers adorned the exhibition room with a few palm trees and garden chairs, the kind you could easily find in a real *jardin d'hiver* (winter garden).

This atmospheric *Verfremdung* of the exhibition hall evokes an infinitely subtle

behavioural change in the spectator, fills him or her, for a moment, with a sense of finding him- or herself in a botanic garden or a science museum. Without really noticing it, the spectator of the artwork briefly takes leave of his or her role, no longer tries to find the message conveyed by the work before his or her eyes, and forgets the question 'What is the artist trying to say to us'. Instead the spectator begins to take an interest, with unprejudiced curiosity, in the information about botany and zoology – already oblivious of the fact that he had actually come to contemplate the artworks.

This subliminal behavioural change, caused by the situational use of atmospheric codes, so superbly exercised by Broodthaers, is the decisive effect of what we would like to call atmosphering, as opposed to programming. Atmosphering makes it possible to change a situation effectively without entering into an open conflict with the customary expectations of the spaces involved. Allotment Athletica formulates this overlapping of realities most strikingly: the actual effect of the track is, in the first instance, that pedestrians and drivers behave differently from the way they would behave in an ordinary suburban street. For both use the track, even if they do so on lanes of different materials: cars proceed on the outer lane of red Tarmac, pedestrians run on the inner lane made of rubber (the same material is used for an athletics track proper).

The difference between this and a normal street is that the pedestrian and car lanes are not sectionally separated by a step. Moving on the same plane of action, both parties must be much more considerate of each other. Drivers will drive more slowly, also because, on this surface normally used by human beings (the athletes), a car inevitably feels somewhat out of place. For pedestrians the track offers more possibilities than a normal pavement, if only because the springy rubber flooring feels different to walk on than hard asphalt and correspondingly suggests different actions. And probably the track even transmits a little of that notorious community spirit of sports in the street – which might significantly alter the notion of public space in a suburb. ᴆ

Landed Square

Largely an area of transit, public space in a suburban context has very different connotations and functions to that of urban squares or parks. In the park-and-ride terminal in Hoenheim-Nord, Strasbourg, designed by Zaha Hadid Architects, the various flows come to a hold before moving on in other directions. **Ilka and Andreas Ruby** describe the interrelationship of this public hub with its suburban surroundings.

The building is something that
lowers itself onto the ground from
above rather than growing out
of the earth. It lands. The act
of landing causes a topographical
reorganisation of the ground out
of which the building is developed.

**Zaha Hadid Architects,
Terminus Hoenheim-Nord,
Strasbourg, France, 2001**
Project architect: Stephane Hof
Design team: Stephane Hof,
Sara Klomps, Woody KT Yao,
Sonia Villaseca
Project team: Silvia Forliati,
Patrik Schumacher, Markus
Dochantschi, David Salazar,
Caroline Voet, Eddie Can,
Stanley Lau, Davied Gerber,
Chris Dopheide

Opening page
Usually disregarded as sheer
infrastructure, the parking
here is celebrated as a
genuine form of public space,
akin to an important plaza in
a city. For this is the place
where the public happens to
occur – people coming from
all over the region by different
means of transportation to
'check in' to the city.

Previous page, top
The 'terminus' accommodates
the waiting areas of both tram
and bus stations, plus bicycle
parking. Less than building,
the elevated roof is in fact
nothing but a folded-up
continuation of the ground
plane in the air. At the place
where the tram wagons halt,
the roof place is cut out, as
if rendered superfluous by
the roofs of the trams.

Previous page, bottom
View of the ensemble looking
south. The park-and-ride
facility at the northern edge
of Strasbourg is a traffic hub
between car, train, tram and
bus traffic-flows. Set amidst
a typically suburban patchwork
of housing, allotments,
production facilities and
agricultural fields, it creates
a coherence out of the
heterogenous adjacencies.

One of the red threads in Zaha Hadid's oeuvre is to conceive of a building not as an isolated object but as a result of a broader manipulation of the topography of the site. Generally this manipulation is conducted from a bird's-eye vantage point, which stages the ground as a gigantic mass. At the same time the bird's-eye view suggests that the building is something that lowers itself onto the ground from above rather than growing out of the earth. It lands. The act of landing causes a topographical reorganisation of the ground out of which the building is developed. Its origins in its spatial context often remain hidden, as in most cases only the building itself is given a designed form, while the surrounding external space remains untouched.

In Strasbourg, Hadid was eventually able to expose the often-concealed manner in which her architecture charges (and, in turn, is charged by) its surroundings. Here, the building itself – a folded roof sheltering people waiting for trams and buses from the elements – forms but one part of the project; the other part is the infrastructural landscape of the generously laid-out parking plane. The parking spaces are graphically defined by white lines painted on the ground and inclined lampposts to light the space at night. In addition, the parking surface, made of dark asphalt, is interrupted by a monumental graphic figure cast in a lighter concrete.

Seen from the perspective of a pedestrian, its significance is not entirely clear. Its actual shape is revealed only from a bird's-eye view, the light concrete figure on the ground seamlessly continued in the roof of the waiting area. The traditional urban space dichotomy between figure (built) and ground (nonbuilt) dissolves as the building's footprint is seamlessly absorbed by the overall form of the ground. Thanks to the omission of actual exterior walls, the waiting area does not read as a 'building' but rather as an elevated replica of the ground plane below.

Inversely, the actual ground is not rendered as an absence (of building). It continues the built volume of the shelter in the 'ghost volume' of the parking plane produced by the inclined lampposts which, in fact, mimics the inclination of the terminal roof and its vertical supports. The aerial view, visually suggestive of a plan, finally reveals that the phenomenological complexity that the car park unfolds at ground level, with its forest of lines and points, is, in fact, based on a rather simple geometric pattern that appears to transfer Walter de Maria's 'Lightning Field' to Strasbourg in a single graceful movement.

In Hadid's project, the Land Art approach to space is translated into a space-making strategy that seems perfectly apt for a suburban condition. It allows her to embrace the flatness of suburbia and to actively explore it. She does not even try to domesticate its *terrain vague* with the vertical way to build space common to classical urbanism – that is, by creating a square type of space through facades that are oriented to one another. For in suburbia this approach would be doomed, as it does not produce new space, but only one more object – something suburbia is not exactly short of. What it does lack, however, are spaces that interconnect existing objects and their spatial peripheries.

In suburbia, public space – a principal ambition of the project – has to be open enough to tie in adjacent open spaces. And it is this 'coherency potential' that could be regarded as the genuine quality of Terminus Hoenheim-Nord in terms of (sub)urbanism. Its carefully laid-out emptiness creates a magnetic field that binds the various programmes of the context – single-family houses, allotments, industrial sheds, trams, streets and railway – together into one single entity, animated by the flows of buses, trams, cars, trains and pedestrians. If looking for a kind of public space in suburbia that is not, for once, produced by the mechanic (mis)application of urban typologies but through the conceptual refinement of its inherent specificities, then one is likely to find it in Strasbourg's Hoenheim-Nord. Δ

Beware, Objects in Suburbia May Be Closer Than They Appear!

At the periphery, where single unrelated objects designed for the passing driver alternate with vast expanses of land, scale and distance become crucial to spatial experience. **Ilka and Andreas Ruby** observe how Lyons Architects used their Sunshine Hospital extension to reorganise the perceptual landscape of a suburban site at the very edge of Greater Melbourne.

In many of their projects, Lyons Architects address the suburban condition of Australia's metropolitan areas. As opposed to the exotic cliché propelled by a certain school of Australian architecture that has idealised the Australian outback as the natural habitat of the fifth continent, most of its inhabitants actually live in the big coastal metropolitan zones. Throughout the past decades, big cities like Melbourne and Sydney have sprawled intensely, which has made their peripheries outgrow their historical downtowns by far. The area of Greater Melbourne, for example, has meanwhile reached the size of the territory of Los Angeles, with a similarly small downtown and a seemingly endless carpet of low-density settlement around it.

Sunshine Hospital is situated at the very edge of this carpet, in the middle of not nothing, but surely of not very much, which makes it easy to discern for the driver-by. The project consists of two separate buildings of different sizes and programme: a larger ward building and a smaller hydrotherapy building. With their intense orange and yellow coloured surfaces

Lyons Architects, Sunshine
Hospital, St Albans, Victoria,
Australia, 2001
Design team: Corbett Lyon,
Cameron Lyon, Carey Lyon, Neil
Appleton, Peter Bartlett, Robert
Tursi, Miles Lauritz, Barbara
Bamford, Chris Downing

Opposite, top
Sunshine Hospital plays with the
scalelessness of the suburban
context at the western edge of
metropolitan Melbourne. The
peculiar properties of the
suburban territory – the
incoherence of its fabric and the
loose positioning of its built
structures within a vast open
space – question architecture's
sovereignty over territory.

Opposite, bottom
The three rows of punched
windows do not, in fact, stand for
three separate storeys; the space
inside – the hydrotherapy pool – is
one continuous volume, punctured
by small rectangular openings
that only from the outside look
like windows (outside again, we
register that some of the windows
are in fact only square shapes
rendered in black brick).

Above right
Both buildings have facades
of coloured bricks laid in a
figurative manner that seems to
picture the visual effect of the
setting sun on the buildings. The
surface pattern has a strangely
despatialising effect, reminiscent
of the 'dazzle paintings' invented
during the First World War to
protect ships against predatory
submarines.

Below right
The replicating relationship with
the larger building does not stop at
the question of scale, as it also
clones the visual effects of some of
the latter's three-dimensional
spatial properties. As such the
cantilevering porch and the set-
back corner are replicated by
mimicking their assumed shadows.

Note
1 See Albert Roskam, 'Dazzle
painting: art as camouflage –
camouflage as art, *Daidalos* 51,
1994, pp 110–15. What
differentiates the dazzle painting
from a conventional camouflage is
the fact that it does not operate
through an assimilation of figure to
background. Instead it creates a
blurring effect inside the figure
itself, which is why it could be
called an intensive camouflage.

aggressively challenging the mellow tones of the
sparse bush vegetation, the buildings virtually
shoot out of their context. But while one can
grasp them from far away, it seems difficult to
precisely locate them in space.

Both buildings have facades of coloured
bricks laid in a figurative manner that seems to
picture the effect of the setting sun (a pictorial
allusion to the euphemistic name of the hospital,
the location of which, in reality, is one of the
socially less bright neighbourhoods of Greater
Melbourne). The pattern on their surface has a
strangely despatialising effect. It seems to play
a constant cat-and-mouse game with our visual
perception, as if resisting being pinned down.
One is reminded of the dazzle paintings invented
during the First World War to protect ships
against predatory submarines. Painting the ships
with perceptually confusing patterns (based
on the techniques of false perspective, figure-
ground conflicts and scale inversions) made
it difficult for submarines' torpedo crews to
determine either the contours or the direction
in which the ship was heading.[1] Along the same
lines, Lyons' buildings appear to swim in their
context like a lone dazzle-painted ship at sea –
omnipresent yet continually out of reach.

This ambition, to create an uncertainty about
the buildings' location in space (as this space
itself is highly uncertain), guides the architectural
concept of the project as well. Our scale
apprehension is systematically misguided by a
cunning manipulation of the scale relationship
between the two buildings. Standing in front of
the main ward building, we see the hydrotherapy
building in the background and are ready to take it
for a more or less exact copy of the first building.
What we don't yet know is that it is, in fact, a 50
per cent replica and that it hence appears to be
standing much further away than it actually is.

We get the first clue only as we cross the parking
square and move into the deceptive depth of the territory.
Viewed from the side, the previously more distanced
hydrotherapy building shifts in the foreground and
appears to be equal in size to the (actually bigger) ward
building in the background. But why does it have such
a monstrosity for a roof? We finally get the hidden logic
of the scale manipulation: the three rows of punched
windows do not, in fact, stand for three separate storeys;
the space inside – the hydrotherapy pool – is one
continuous volume, punctured by small rectangular
openings that only from the outside look like windows
(outside again, we register that some of the windows
are in fact only square shapes rendered in black brick).

Yet the replicating relationship with the larger building
does not stop at the question of scale. For it also clones
the visual effects of some of the latter's three-
dimensional spatial properties. As such the cantilevering
porch and the set-back corner are replicated by
mimicking their assumed shadows. Soon we are
immersed in a relentless play of multiple reproductions.
If the first building only reproduces the effect of a setting
sun on its facade, the second replicates the first building
altogether, including both the applied facade image
and the visual effect of the building itself.

While this copying technique addresses the repetitive
character of the suburban built environment, the scale
manipulation plays with the overwhelming scalelessness
of the suburban context. The peculiar properties of the
suburban territory – the incoherence of its fabric and
the loose positioning of its built structures within vast
open space – question the capability of architecture
to organise the territory. In fact, it feels much more
the other way around: the territory conditions the
performance of architecture. And this could well be
a lesson to learn from suburbia. ∆

Creating the

When something is planned in suburbia, it generally takes the form of monofunctional developments: residential settlements, business parks, shopping centres or the like. Very rarely these programmes appear in mixed configurations – as if their combination would be to their disadvantage. As a consequence, the territorial continuity of suburbia is more often than not fragmented into an archipelago of enclaves that do not communicate one with another. They are never close enough to create that productive friction that makes one plus one equal three. With the 'in-between' as a dormant condition, hardly any programmatic synergies can occur.

  This is the condition the projects assembled in this section try to influence. All start from one particular programme but attempt to put it in relationship with other activities. As such the Italian office of Metrogramma explores the potential of congesting suburban uses (traditionally

In-Between

organised on only one floor) by devising infrastructural hubs that accommodate multiple parties and uses. In this way, development costs for each of them are reduced as well as the consumption of land surface that is scarce in the Alpine city of Bolzano, in Italy. In other conditions, where space is available, the activation of the so far mainly unused space in between existing structures becomes the focus of intervention. For example, Slovenian architects Sadar Vuga propose to upgrade a suburban agglomeration of shopping boxes by equipping the network of car-only access roads between them with a pedestrian circulation system raised off the ground, and additional programmes enlivening the site even after shopping hours. Swiss architects EM2N invert the negative space in between a surreal puzzle of typical suburban uses into a positive space by reprogramming it into a park that enacts the spatial connection between the hitherto dissociated infrastructures.

Sub-Park

How do you go about developing a park as a new magnet for people, investors and new programmes – a central public space within a suburban patchwork of infrastructure, traffic and public utilities? **Daniel Niggli** and **Mathias Müller** of EM2N Architects, and **Lukas Schweingruber** of Zulauf Seippel Schweingruber (zss) landscape architects, describe why it was just this diversity in a site near Zurich that they saw as a quality to be intensified. Instead of adding merely another element to the heterogenous condition, their Glattpark performs an adhesive action, realising the simultaneous existence of different programmes, styles and user groups.

EM2N Architects in association with Zulauf Seippel Schweingruber (zss) landscape architects and Schälchli, Abegg + Hunziker engineers, Glattpark, Zurich and Opfikon, 2002 Design team: Johannes Abegg, Bernd Druffel, Fabian Hoermann, Mathias Müller, Daniel Niggli, Jaqueline Noa, Lukas Schweingruber, Vincent Traber, Rainer Zulauf

Above
The Glatt valley is dominated by a patchwork of infrastructure and public utilities. Crossing linear elements such as train lines, the highway, expressways and the Glatt river are cutting it into heterogenous pieces.

Right, top and bottom
The main intervention of the project is the design of the in-between space with pedestrian circulation, placed in public green space, which gives the park its identity. The functional islands in between are inserted objects (both infrastructural and ecological), which seamlessly marry the artificial and natural to a new synthetic authenticity of a truly suburban public landscape.

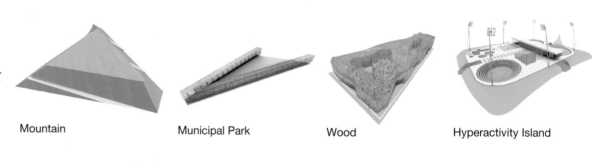

Mountain   Municipal Park   Wood   Hyperactivity Island

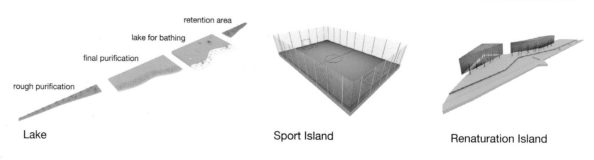

retention area

lake for bathing

final purification

rough purification

Lake   Sport Island   Renaturation Island

The architectural critic Roemer van Toorn talks about a change we are undergoing, away from a society of 'either/or' to a society of 'and'. The prevalent ideas of the 'either/or' society, such as specialisation, transparency and polarity (city/countryside, east/west and so on) are being replaced by concepts like multiculture, paradox, chaos, uncertainty, networks, ambiguity. The 'and' society also moves away from traditional lifestyles and conventions. Previously unthinkable combinations of lifestyles are now becoming possible and accepted. Each individual can collage his or her own world from absolute opposite ways of life and simultaneously live in very different worlds.

Parallel to these developments, the spatial, functional and sociological structures of the traditional city are more or less abolished in suburban conditions. Programmatically as well as morphologically, these conditions are characterised by combinations of elements that you would hardly find in the traditional city.

With its patchwork of infrastructure and public utilities, the Glatt Valley, on the periphery of Zurich, presents a prototypical example of this new (sub)urban condition. Crossing linear elements, such as train lines, the highway, expressways and the Glatt river itself, are cutting the valley into heterogenous pieces. These are occupied by utilities including sewage works, a rubbish-disposal plant, civil-defence training grounds, allotments, sports complexes and woods.

The introduction of the Glattpark as a magnet for new investors and a central public space within this condition leads to a reversal of the valley's settlement logic. The former periphery becomes a new centre of gravity, and hitherto forgotten in-between spaces turn into vital places of the surrounding agglomeration. The Glatt river, today a polluted ditch, evolves into the new spatial and atmospheric backbone of the valley. Previously avoided non-places, such as sewage works, are put in context with their surroundings and start to perform as new attractors for future development.

It is clearly the juxtaposition of its various elements, with their different uses and atmospheres, that makes the Glatt valley an exciting place. Therefore, colonising the 'wild' industrial nature of the area with a preconceived notion of a 'park' harboured the risk of installing the backward utopia of a leisure idyll, compensating for the perceived deficits of the periphery with an ecological patch. To embrace the potential of the area, it was crucial that the park be developed from the existing conditions, for example by accepting the dominance of infrastructure elements and the juxtaposition of different programmes. In other words, the success of transforming this 'in-between city' into a new 'city' of the Glatt valley depended on making use of the visible traces of its material history.

The park, as a central public space of the Glatt valley, is intended to appeal to various user groups. It is conceived as a collage of different parts. The multitude of partial public domains and parallel worlds coexist and communicate with each other. Its identity is created through the heterogeneity and difference of its parts. It reinterprets the existing peripheral 'junk programmes' and turns the supposed problem of the dispersed, conflict-laden peripheral conditions into a quality: a tense, almost absurd opposition of different programmes.

The peripheral park is, first and foremost, a connecting machine, an infrastructural web of pathways in between which anything is possible. This action space becomes the equivalent of what in the city would be called public space – something which, in suburbia, is usually forgotten or even purposely given up. Both strategies – the reinterpretation of what appear to be disadvantages into potential, and the reprogramming of infrastructure as public space – are procedures that enable the work of EM2N/ZSS to succeed in places where traditional architectural means are bound to fail. ∆

Congesting the Edge Between City and Landscape

The Italian city of Bolzano is growing but, as its mountainous topography limits its expansion, sprawl is not an option and concepts of densification are vital for future development. Taking the needs of suburban programmes, such as commercial buildings, warehouses and parking space, and mixing them with residential and leisure facilities, **Andrea Boschetti** and **Alberto Francini** of architectural practice Metrogramma discover the potential of infrastructure becoming architecture.

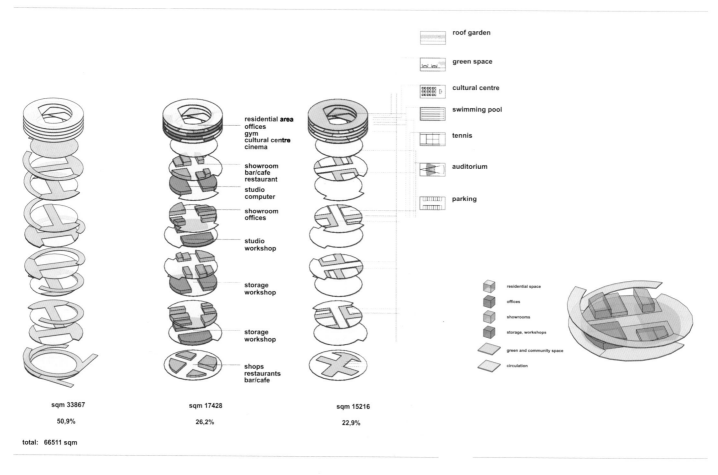

roof garden

green space

cultural centre

swimming pool

tennis

auditorium

parking

residential **area**
offices
gym
cultural centre
cinema

showroom
bar/cafe
restaurant

studio
computer

showroom
offices

studio
workshop

storage
workshop

storage
workshop

shops
restaurants
bar/cafe

residential space

offices

showrooms

storage, workshops

green and community space

circulation

sqm 33867	sqm 17428	sqm 15216
50,9%	26,2%	22,9%

total: 66511 sqm

Superinfrastructure explores and tries to overcome the kern problem of a too broad use of territory working on the extra-large scale of the architectural standard object.

Pathology

The main problems, found in Bolzano as well as in many other current productive settlements, can be summarised as follows:

1 Widespread settlement fragmentation due to small-size parcel allotments and consequent space dispersion.

2 Too cumbersome vertical connections compared to plane surfaces, and the consequent dissipation of usable volume.

3 An inadequate number of parking areas in relation to the number of companies per allotment.

4 Widespread type-morphological unhomogeneity and the consequent 'Disneyland effect'.

5 Functional and logistic incompatibility in the same productive reality.

Treatment

• Macro-parcel allotment to optimise space use and allow cubature.

• New opportunities for plot occupation as associated productive condominiums.

• Sharing of vertical mobility systems and the consequent saving of cubature, costs and infrastructures.

• Adequate numbers of parking areas for the number of companies located in the productive plot.

• High-grade functional mixture.

• Construction according to functional compatibility criteria.

• More public parks, gardens and collective spaces enabling a higher quality of life and work.

Three Settlement Principles of High Density: Point, Line, Surface

The standard productive condominium, nothing new yet still in need of re-examining, seemed to be the best reference model in order to answer the problems cited above. On an extra-large scale it has the remarkable ability of absorbing considerable quantities of cubature in fewer surfaces, of reducing economic investments and of stimulating new relations between public and private projects.

Metrogramma therefore conceived a 'productive prototype', out of which they let emerge three superinfrastructural types.

The prototype conceptualises the congestion subject and expresses the ambition of planning a

Metrogramma,
Superinfrastructure research project for the city Bolzano, Italy, 2003
Design team: Andrea Boschetti, Alberto Francini with Enzo Fontana, Soik Jung, Marco Baccarelli, Eugenio Morello, Tomohiro Yanagisawa

Opposite and right
A double system of helicoidal slopes allows the separation of cars and customer traffic from goods transport and internal services. Therefore, different floors alternate between warehouses, laboratories and garages to spaces much more suitable for selling, display and contact with customers. A constructional principle can thus develop storehouse levels into a structural floor.

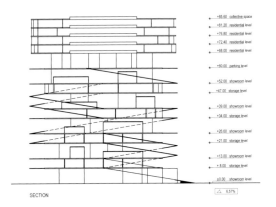

SECTION

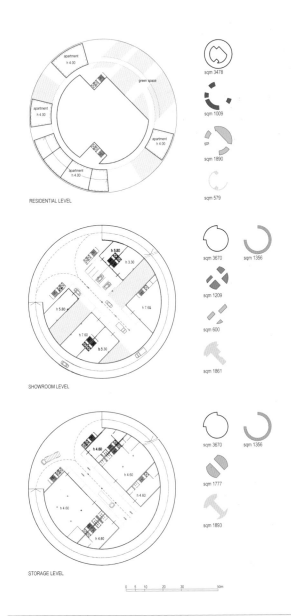

RESIDENTIAL LEVEL

SHOWROOM LEVEL

STORAGE LEVEL

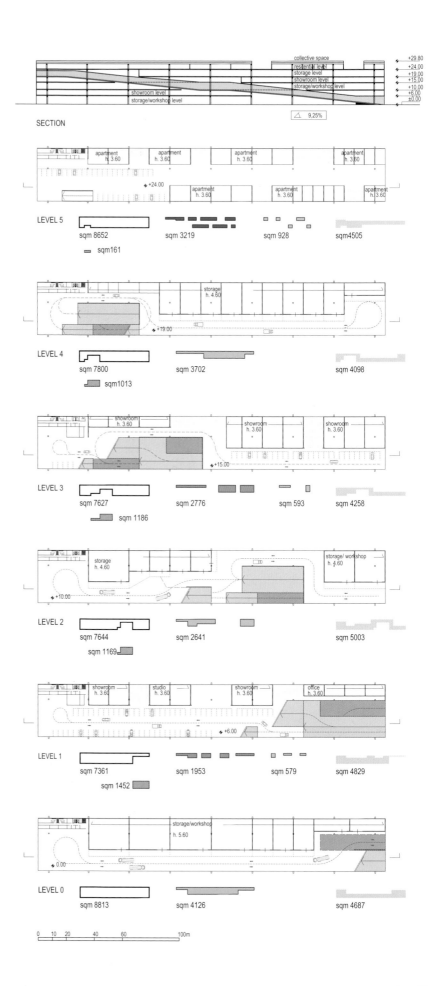

SECTION

△ 9,25%

LEVEL 5

sqm 8652   sqm 3219   sqm 928   sqm4505

sqm161

LEVEL 4

sqm 7800   sqm 3702   sqm 4098

sqm1013

LEVEL 3

sqm 7627   sqm 2776   sqm 593   sqm 4258

sqm 1186

LEVEL 2

sqm 7644   sqm 2641   sqm 5003

sqm 1169

LEVEL 1

sqm 7361   sqm 1953   sqm 579   sqm 4829

sqm 1452

LEVEL 0

sqm 8813   sqm 4126   sqm 4687

0 10 20   40   60   100m

Right and opposite
The street structure takes to
the extreme the idea of the
inhabited road. The street
loses its traditional
bi-dimensional logic and in
itself becomes a generating
womb of space and complexity.
About 250 small and middle-
size companies could find
space inside this volume, the
minimum dimensions of which
would be 245 metres long by
36 metres wide.

structure in the form of a city, which is still synthesised with its main features (both in public and private plans) in a sole volume.

This prototype consists of three remarkable architectural objects, still abstract and vague in form and materials, but motionless from the spatial and perceptive point of view – three huge overscale objects able to guarantee to the multitude of companies contained in it the largest visibility and promotional autonomy.

This is an XL product that shows in different forms verticalisation of infrastructures inside these remarkable urban realities; high-density structures, at least in their conceptual simplicity, identified according to three different settlement principles: point (tower structure), line (street structure) and surface (slab structure).

Each type occupies a hectare (10,000 square metres) of property and is able to contain a number of companies. According to current criteria and urban regulations of the province of Bolzano, this is equal to a corresponding 100,000-square-metre occupation of the territory.

Living in the Air: the Tower Structure

Metrogramma's first meta-project gives birth to considerations on the subject of vertical density, in which collective spaces, multicompany divisions, warehouses, parking areas, residential zones and services of various natures, merge into a sole 'urban event', which has a maximum height of 90 metres. This 'tower' superinfrastructure takes to the extreme the idea of vertical mobility, which lifts the city and its services to a higher level.

Overall dimensions are still the minimum necessary surface according to profit and cost estimation. The circular tower diameter is, in this case, 100 metres, which allows gentle slopes for every means of transport on wheels, and easy handling within the productive condominium.

A double system of helicoidal slopes allows the separation of car- and customer-traffic from goods transport and internal services. Therefore, different floors alternate between warehouses, laboratories and garages as spaces much more suitable for selling, display and contact with customers. Thus, a constructional principle can develop storehouse levels into a structural floor.

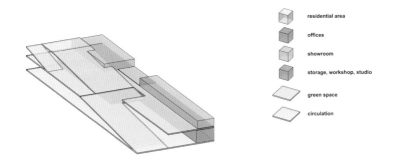

residential area
offices
showroom
storage, workshop, studio
green space
circulation

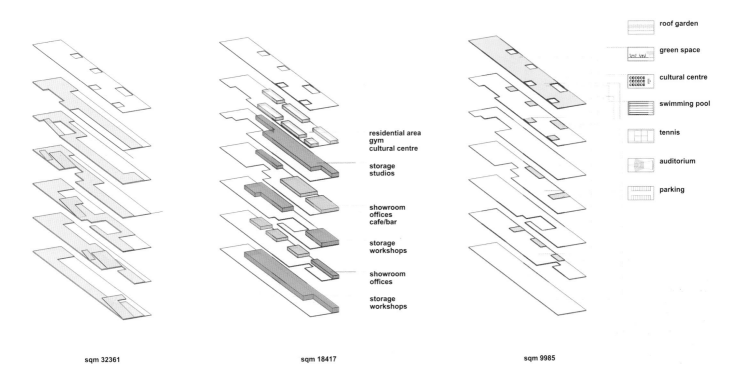

roof garden
green space
cultural centre
swimming pool
tennis
auditorium
parking

residential area
gym
cultural centre

storage
studios

showroom
offices
cafe/bar

storage
workshops

showroom
offices

storage
workshops

sqm 32361

53,3%

sqm 18417

30,3%

sqm 9985

16,4%

total: 60763 sqm = 100%

Offices, residential zones and general collective services – such as kindergartens, fitness areas, swimming pools, playgrounds and restaurants – are located at the higher levels. All of the areas inside the tower superinfrastructure are thought, at least partly, to be an internal ecological oasis in the productive event.

In this sense, the whole complex has been planned not as a big air-conditioned case, but as an infrastructural vertical frame, which can be progressively colonised and apportioned by different companies.

According to urban scale, 'tower' absorbs considerable portions of territory, returning areas of open spaces to the city.

Living the Infrastructure: the Street Structure

This second type of project explores the subject of longitudinal density, in which collective spaces, multicompany divisions, warehouses, parking areas, residential zones and services of various natures merge into a sole 'urban event', which endlessly develops in length, taking advantage of the proximity of roads and large channels of communication.

Street-level superinfrastructure takes to the extreme the idea of inhabited roads. The street loses its traditional bidimensional logic and in itself becomes a generating womb of space and complexity.

Therefore, this concept becomes the opportunity to redefine new interaction possibilities between street network and a complex programme of productive settlements.

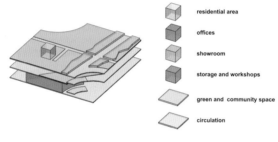

residential area
offices
showroom
storage and workshops
green and community space
circulation

Above left
The towers pop up in the landscape and act as new landmarks in front of the backdrop of the Alpine mountain panorama.

Above right
Taking up the scale of the mountains, the horizontal slab structures both blend and contrast with the generously laid-out valley of Bolzano.

Right and opposite (left)
The slab structure takes to the extreme the idea of a city on superimposed levels. Created from a base module, with minimal dimensions (necessary surface) of 108 metres x 108 metres, and 14 metres in height, this superinfrastructure concentrates the whole vertical ascending system to its epicentre. Open spaces, parking areas, services and gardens could find a new position on the roof of the productive slab condominium, reiterating the building of a new floor at a different height. Thus, a green roof is able to welcome a real new city at low density.

Opposite, top right
The street structure flips the ground surface of the street into elevation and creates a strip of attractions that are accessible from the street.

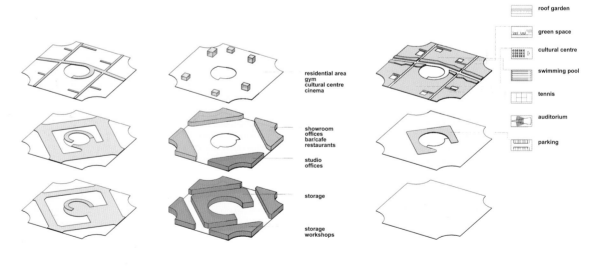

residential area
gym
cultural centre
cinema

showroom
offices
bar/cafe
restaurants

studio
offices

storage

storage
workshops

roof garden
green space
cultural centre
swimming pool
tennis
auditorium
parking

sqm 14362   sqm 9795   sqm 6143

47,4%   32,3%   20,3%

total: 30300 sqm = 100%

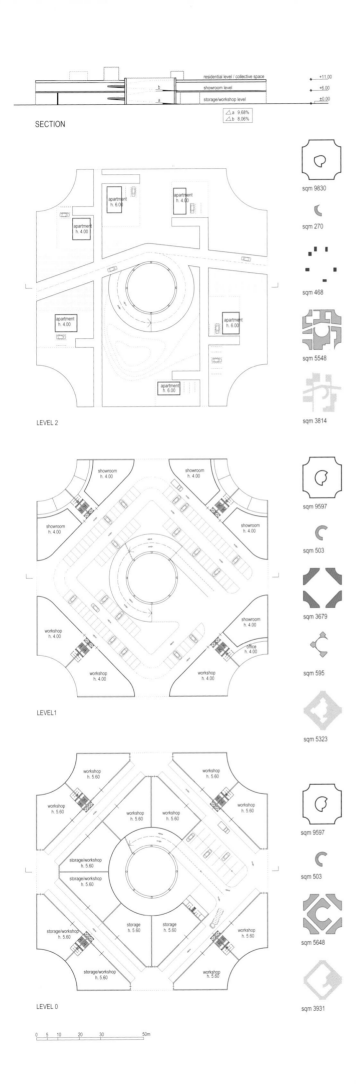

SECTION

residential level / collective space   +11,00
showroom level   +6,00
storage/workshop level   +0,00

△a 9.68%
△b 8.06%

LEVEL 2

sqm 9830

sqm 270

sqm 468

sqm 5548

sqm 3814

apartment h. 6.00
apartment h. 4.00
apartment h. 4.00
apartment h. 4.00
apartment h. 6.00
apartment h. 6.00

LEVEL1

showroom h. 4.00
showroom h. 4.00
showroom h. 4.00
showroom h. 4.00
showroom h. 4.00
office h. 4.00
workshop h. 4.00
workshop h. 4.00
workshop h. 4.00

sqm 9597

sqm 503

sqm 3679

sqm 595

sqm 5323

LEVEL 0

workshop h. 5.60
workshop h. 5.60
workshop h. 5.60
workshop h. 5.60
workshop h. 5.60
storage/workshop h. 5.60
storage/workshop h. 5.60
storage/workshop h. 5.60
storage h. 5.60
storage h. 5.60
workshop h. 5.60
workshop h. 5.60

sqm 9597

sqm 503

sqm 5648

sqm 3931

0 5 10   20   30   50m

Minimum overall dimensions for this superinfrastructure are 245 metres long by 36 metres wide (minimum necessary surface). In fact, this portion of territory coincides with the wide road that rises in height. This size allows easy manoeuvring and U-turns inside the productive condominium. Height is fixed to 24 metres according to the regulations.

The street is a belt that unrolls and climbs diagonally up the whole structure, dividing it into two identical and symmetric sections.

In this case different floors also alternate between warehouses, laboratories and garages as spaces much more suitable for selling, display and contact with customers in general.

Metrogramma has calculated that approximately 250 small and middle-size companies could find space inside this volume.

Living the Landscape: the Slab Structure

The third and final project type raises considerations on the subject of the horizontal density, in which collective spaces, different companies, warehouses, parking areas, residential zones and services of various natures merge into a sole plain, spacious 'urban event' that optimises within a low height the settlement growth of the territory.

The slab structure takes to the extreme the idea of a city on superimposed levels.

Created from a base module, with minimal dimensions (necessary surface) of 108 metres by 108 metres, with a height of 14 metres, this superinfrastructure concentrates the whole vertical ascending system to its epicentre. This slab type is similar to a huge tile, which due to its modularity and potential repetitiveness enables the layout of a whole area of urban landscape.

Open spaces, parking areas, services and gardens (the usual 'urban materials' of the city) can find a new position on the roof of the productive slab condominium, reiterating the building of a new floor at a different height. Thus, a green roof is able to welcome a real new city at low density. Still, its attitude to expansion does not preclude the possibility of a slab-structure project as an 'isolated' urban element, even able to change convert unhomogeneous and untidy plots. ◬

Sub-City:
the Transformation
of a Non-Place

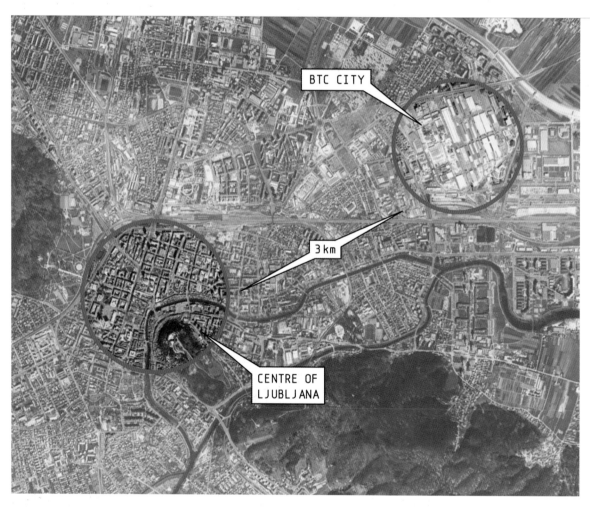

Suburbia sometimes occurs adjacent to the city centre, as is the case with BTC City in Ljubljana, Slovenia. **Bostjan Vuga** of Sadar Vuga Arhitekti takes us on a journey through time, describing the evolution of a suburban shopping city out of an urban blind spot, and its growing ambitions to become a genuine city.

BTC City is the largest Slovenian business-shopping-sports-entertainment centre. Its aim is to become the largest in Europe.

Sadar Vuga Arhitekti in association with Partek, BTC City, Ljubljana, Slovenia, 2003
Design team: (Sadar Vuga Arhitekti) Juri Sadar, Bostjan Vuga, Tomaz Kristof; (Parsek) Andrej Nabergoi, Ozrin Skodic

Opposite and above
The BTC shopping and leisure city has the typical infrastructure, construction and night-and-day look of a suburban commercial development yet lies within the city of Ljubljana, the historical centre of which it equals in size.

Above
Founded in the 1950s as a customs freight terminal, the BTC area was completely isolated from the rest of the city and could only be entered with a passport. After the secession of Slovenia from the rest of the then Yugoslavia in 1991, its huge warehouses were converted into shopping halls with parking spaces in between.

Top right
The existing organisation of programmes and circulation. As BTC City has no pavements but plenty of parking space, its customers have developed a truly car-based shopping behaviour: they park, shop, and drive to the next shopping hall, then start the sequence again. To reduce traffic accidents, the BTC company has recently introduced roundabouts.

Bottom right
Night view over BTC City, with the centre of Ljubljana in the background. At night the still-legible suburban touch of the former warehouse agglomeration is smoothly traded for a more urban ambience. A colourfully lit streetscape stages a particularly active nightlife animated by cinemas, restaurants and bars that are open till late.

The two sentences above represent the situation today and the short-term ambition of the BTC company, owner of the BTC shopping city located in the area between the internal and external ring roads of the city of Ljubljana. The shopping city is equal in size to Ljubljana's city centre, and situated only 3 kilometres away from it. It has an intermediate, hybrid position, and is a shopping city with the typical infrastructure, construction and night-and-day look usually found along major roads on the peripheries of bigger cities. It is a concentrate of the suburban, placed within an urban frame. BTC is an area where urban operativity and imagery overlap the suburban, where the line dividing the typically urban and the typically suburban is being erased, where the conditions are fulfilled so that the BTC shopping city may become the BTC genuine city.

To better understand the genealogy of this miraculous transformation, it is necessary to take a look at how it all started and follow its development up to the present day, before risking a glimpse at its future.

Zooming back to the 1950s, the eastern part of the city now occupied by BTC is a typical industrial area with warehouses and railway freight along the road, today Letaliska Cesta (Airport Road) leading to the city and the runway of the deserted airport. Proletarian suburban houses, smaller housing blocks, patches of green surfaces between rails, and large warehouses and workshops give the area its city-outskirts appearance, and only those living or working here can be found in these completely unattractive suburbs.

This warehouse centre is then developed and expanded, new halls are built and smaller office buildings constructed, providing headquarters for warehouse and distribution companies.

By the mid-1970s, the warehouse centre is serving the needs of the then Yugoslavia as the largest inland customs terminal in Europe. More and more people from other parts of the city are coming to these eastern outskirts, and starting to mix with those working in the customs and duty-free areas. But this inland terminal is a closed area, divided from the rest of the city and entered only with a pass. It is a customs area far away from state borders – a territory embraced with a fence, similar to an airport or military barracks.

As a result of Slovenia's secession from Yugoslavia and its independence from the beginning of the 1990s, as well as the privatisation of social property, the warehouse centre loses its purpose. The big country becomes history and the big government companies are gone, leaving behind only big, unprofitable and half-empty warehouses in this increasingly urbanising eastern suburb. Should the warehouses simply be pulled down to enable the development of new built structures, apartments, business premises and public institutions, which would quickly urbanise the eastern suburbs? Or should they be sold off to various buyers, and the future of the area be left to chance?

Interestingly, the company that owned the warehouse centre remains in operation (though reformed as a limited liability company), and BTC Ltd now owns 200,000 square metres of warehouses, infrastructure and land surrounding the area.

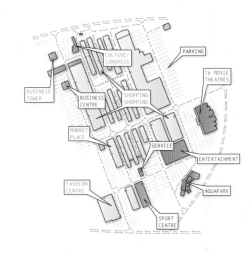

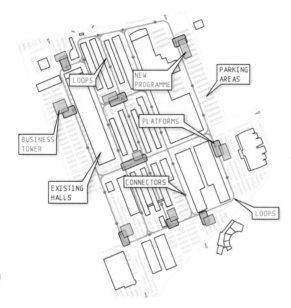

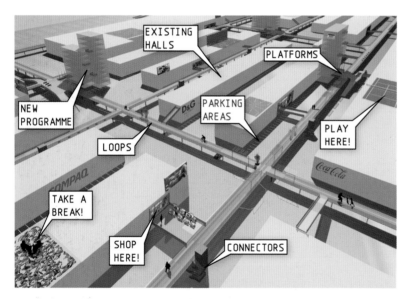

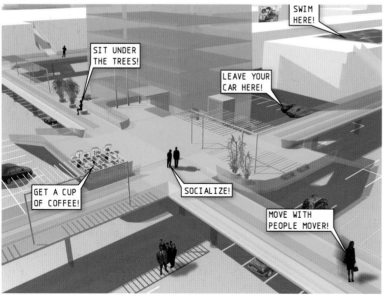

The company takes the decision to transform the warehouse centre and enable every new Slovene capitalist to do what they most want to do: buy, buy, and buy some more. It takes advantage of the existing built structure of the warehouses which, with some cosmetic correction of their interiors and exteriors, begin to serve as places for buying and selling. The generic ground plan, and the height of, and full perimeter walls around the constructions prove ideal for all types of shops, from large supermarkets to small premises that line simple internal streets, and multistorey department stores. The warehouse centre is surreptitiously turning into a shopping centre.

Traffic infrastructure and asphalted functional land around the shopping halls offer parking areas, the convenient delivery of goods and easy access for shoppers. Rents for shopping premises in the renovated warehouses are relatively cheap. Lessees do not have high opening costs, whilst the masses of shoppers, who are suddenly discovering a consumers' paradise in the former grey warehouse zone, promise a quick return on assets and easy profit. As a consequence, the warehouse suburb is becoming a shopping mecca for shoppers from Ljubljana and its surroundings. And as the BTC shopping city borders the already completed external ring road, shoppers are brought even more quickly to the objects of their desire. The city centre is starting to empty, as everything anyone needs or wishes to buy can be found at BTC – even when the shops in the city centre are closed.

Neon signs and interesting facades dress up the blank concrete walls of warehouses surrounded by rows of new cars in the parking areas. The initial quick make-over of the shopping halls, using clumsy and poorly designed boards, improves with increased profits, and the interiors start to more closely resemble shopping malls. Shops selling inferior and cheap items soon fail and are replaced with outlets for more discerning shoppers. As rents increase, the BTC company's profits rise significantly. The BTC shopping city is now on the map, and becoming the fastest developing part of Ljubljana via a genuine evolutionary process. The BTC wants to become a genuine city, and wants to do so on private land.

Simultaneously, the former suburban look of the area in this eastern part of the city is slowly disappearing. However, much is still missing – for example pavements and, other than the parking areas, public space in general. Due to the monofunctional nature of the shopping city, there is no interconnection between programmes, and no further social interaction as activities are limited to shopping. Visitors drive here, park, buy, drive to the next hall, buy something else and drive away. BTC has a generic identity, a generic atmosphere and a generic character for a generic activity – shopping.

Opposite, middle
The new pedestrian
infrastructure enables you to
park your car somewhere and
then move your body. You
become a *flâneur* at BTC, you
start interacting with people.
You rise above the shopping
ground with escalators and
elevators to the system of
bigger and smaller loops,
pedestrian pathways that
spread and interweave across
the entire area.

Opposite, bottom
At crossways the loops spread
to platforms, suspended
gardens of BTC City. Green
surfaces with pavilions are the
centre of the new urban life in
the mezzanine of highly
specialised shops that satisfy
even the most demanding
market groups. Computer-
generated sounds travel and
mix with simulated sounds of
nature from beauty salons,
where platforms are identified
by the smells coming from
pavilions.

Above and next page
Parking areas alongside the
buildings towards the centre of
BTC provide free land for new
buildings. New office towers,
hotels and apartments with
three-storey penthouses,
accessible via the mezzanine,
are growing almost as fast as
the warehouses were being
turned into shopping halls a
little over a decade ago.

But shopping always asks for more. A relatively large area of BTC land remains undeveloped, and a number of old, inappropriately constructed warehouses need to be replaced with new ones, so a second phase of development is launched, destined to increase BTC's degree of urbanity and create the atmosphere and character of a genuine city. New large buildings increas the range on offer at BTC, and shopping is complemented with entertainment. Thus it is at BTC where Slovenia's first big multiplex is built, followed by a congress hall and a theatre.

Shopping also embraces sports and fitness, hence a new, glass, fitness centre is constructed, along with covered tennis courts. And shopping is also a natural magnet for business, so the BTC company builds an office tower for housing its headquarters and for renting out space to foreign companies looking for modern business premises with quick and easy access as well as their own parking spaces.

We now enter the last years of the second millennium. Increasing profits pay for the replacement of old halls with new buildings for shopping malls over several storeys. These are more sophisticated and more glamorous than the previous ones, with bigger signs and glazed surfaces. The former warehouses are beginning

to open and communicate with the public infrastructure. Trees are planted, streetlights begin to appear, and there is even a promenade connecting two of the larger halls. Next comes an outdoor market selling fruit and vegetables, and a belvedere restaurant at the top of the office tower. Public buses provide a connection to the city centre.

BTC's ambition to become a genuine city is becoming increasingly visible, and the city authorities begin to point a finger at BTC, claiming it is emptying the shops in the old centre, that hardly anyone is using the existing cinema, and that new bars and nightclubs are being opened in BTC and not in the city centre. They reproach BTC, the former grey warehouse suburban zone, for its most characteristic feature – its urbanity.

Whilst the city centre enjoys its unchangeable state of mediocrity as a two-day tourist attraction, and is beautiful, has an identity, an atmosphere and a character, in contrast BTC is not beautiful, has no identity, no atmosphere and no character. But the company has ambitions, capital and the will to acquire whatever it takes to become a city. Ultimately, it is urban planner and investor in conjunction.

Today BTC is a place for shopping, doing business, exercising, watching films, eating, holding meetings and so on. A large aquapark with 2,000 square metres of open and covered swimming pools, an entertainment centre with a casino and a new sports complex are now being built. A second, taller office tower is also planned,

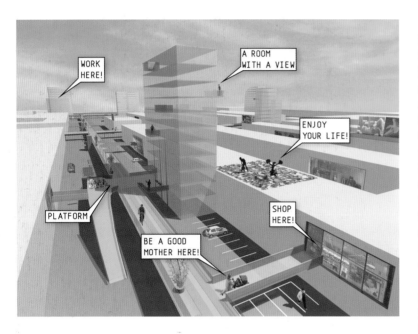

To begin to answer these questions, we might fast-forward in time to the year 2012. BTC City has just won the award for the most beautifully laid-out new European city. At the same time, the company witnesses a record number of overnight stays at two hotels in its area. Here, guests on business trips can find everything they need: off-line and on-line architecture, which helps them manage their time efficiently, so as much as possible can be spent pursuing pleasure activities. BTC City is becoming a pleasure city, the design and operativity of which is guided by the principles of leisure urbanity. And as a result, Ljubljana is becoming one of the few non-resort places in Europe where pleasure and amusement are the main identity parameters. BTC City has become a vehicle for branding the city of Ljubljana, on a par with the historical centre and Ljubljana Castle.

BTC City is also recording a considerable growth in population. If the current trend continues, in around three years as many people will live in the elegant Spa Towers as in the city centre. Living in BTC City has become a status symbol. Efficient advertising campaigns around the world have increased the prices of duplexes and triplexes in the towers, which are attracting local metromen and global urban nomads, as do those in other European cities. The lower floors of Spa Towers have grooming rooms, areas for the relaxation of body and soul, which afford opportunities to meet and to socialise, 24 hours a day, 365 days a year, and spread from the tower interiors to pavilions on the green platforms of the mezzanine.

The mezzanine forms a system of loops and platforms, linked to the shopping ground with vertical connectors. It is raised above the shopping ground, is completely green and is intended only for pedestrians and cyclists. The shopping ground remains below, as it was 20 years ago. It still offers a wide range of goods, available to all. And there are still direct entrances to the sports, entertainment, cultural and business facilities from the parking areas.

Whoever wants more, goes higher. The mezzanine hosts top-end specialist retail outlets. Here, the individual mixes with the global, the computer-generated sounds spread from loudspeakers and mix with simulated sounds of nature from beauty salons, and platforms are identified by the smells coming from pavilions.

BTC City is becoming a world of new, controlled, visual, sound and haptic impulses. It seems to react to one's mood, generating a perfect interaction. For was it not the synergy between the on-line and off-line architecture of BTC City that enabled you to meet your partner on the mezzanine a year ago? A relaxing sound from your mobile announced that on the parallel loop, three sequences away, there was a person, who most matched the profile description of your desired partner. The two of you met and had a drink in one of grooming rooms.

BTC City is pure mental luxury. ⏃

though it is as yet unclear whether it will house just offices or a hotel as well. Due to the constant growth of capital in BTC, development is gradually covering all available land with new building.

The former warehouse centre, now transformed into a shopping-business-entertainment centre, is frantically 'playing city'. A growing number of people spend their time here, on weekdays and at the weekend, not only throughout the day but also after hours, in the restaurants and bars which, at dusk, become animated with various colours. Yet despite all this, there is still a touch of the suburbs at BTC, because one always goes there with a purpose – to shop, have fun, exercise, work – but never only to walk or as a *flâneur*. People do not meet their friends here before deciding where to go for a drink. The duration of one's stay at BTC is defined by the duration of one's purpose.

Clearly, BTC is still not a genuine city (though last year it appeared in a book of the country's cities as the only new Slovene city!). But why does it want to become one in the first place? Is it looking for a means of increasing profits once the extensive development and occupation of available land within its own territory has come to an end? How can it encourage people to come here without a purpose, and make them stay and interact among themselves? Would this increased degree of urbanity bring BTC mentally closer to the city centre? Would Ljubljana then have two centres, the old and the new downtowns? Would there be synergy between them. Will they complete each other? Will both centres raise the urban attraction of Ljubljana?

Below
Limiting the palette of materials reinforces the bold, easily legible forms.
Here the arcade acts to gather people from a rather weak conjunction of
routes and focus them towards the foyer.

Theatre,
Chigwell School

Below left
Site plan. The drama centre sits at one edge of the school's site.

Below right
Ground-floor plan. Ancillary accommodation wraps around two sides of the main auditorium, functionally and symbolically uniting teaching and drama.

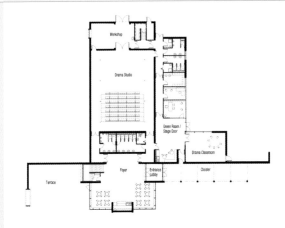

The prospect of viewing a new theatre by Arts Team @ RHWL takes **Jeremy Melvin** on his push-bike through the Waltham Marshes to Woodford. It proves to be a John Betjeman-like encounter with suburbia, in which Melvin must pass through miles of ribbon roads and faceless residential streets before emerging in the verdant enclave of Chigwell School. Once there he encounters a 'bold and unfussy work of architecture', with a creative take on the needs of a school-level drama facility.

As you travel out of London the suburbs become more standard and duller: the further you are from the centre the more they appear to merge into the same greyness that seems to render Purley indistinguishable from Plaistow, or Sutton from Southgate. Eventually the banality overwhelms any connection with your means of transport and your senses focus in on themselves as if you were reading a catalogue – of suburbia. One section tells you of the newest and sweetest thing in lace curtains; another which fast motorcars go with which atrophied caricatures of familiar architectural features. A third might suggest a choice of road names. Replication grants a kind of authenticity to imperial connections like Mafeking, Quebec or Jubilee; bird names like grebe, cormorant or sandpiper are a common standby. If these don't appeal, what about Oxford University colleges like Balliol or Merton, as much to do with their landowning tentacles as academic ambitions of suburb planners? But passing through the ribbon roads linking the various villages that constitute London, one question grows to dwarf all others: when will it END? I know. I've been there. It's called Chigwell. And I have returned with a story to tell.

Passing from the sterility of Woodford, across the M11 motorway, one enters a locality where, as if in a dream, the shrivelled architectural ornaments of the earlier neighbourhoods unwind to something beyond full size; the driveways do not seem crowded even if they have half a dozen soft-topped Mercedes and a score of four-by-fours. Beyond this realm of gigantism there be not hippogriffs but a sort of Shangri-La where, judging by its sign, the local pub is named after the one king who lost his head – literally. A few years before that event the local vicar, whose ambitions later took him to the archbishopric of York, founded a grammar school whose original buildings, along with the pub and church, create a village centre where time might have stopped at the fall of the royal headsman's axe.

But academic institutions can't stand still. Like so many of its counterparts, Chigwell School marks its evolution in a sequence of architectural idioms. Its 17th-century hall has spawned progeny in each subsequent century, always of an indelibly institutional flavour and varying in quality, though spared the worst excesses of design-and-build classrooms, which step tentatively from the inner core across the playing fields towards the distant metropolitan wen.

One end of the campus has a surprise – a bold, unmistakably modern form whose shape and accoutrements would not be out of place in a more urban setting. Certainly it lends urbanity to a point where the school might seep away into the nether

Top left
First-floor plan.

Bottom left
Cross section.

Top right
Long section.

Bottom right
Elevation.

A gallery running around all four sides of the auditorium reinforces the potential to adapt to any configuration. Flexibility becomes a didactic tool.

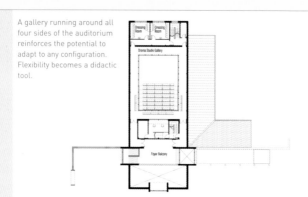

A generous foyer and provision of backstage workshop both strengthen the sense of being a real theatre and double up as teaching spaces.

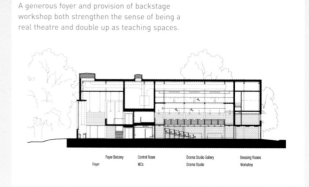

All the basic attributes of a professional theatre are present, at least in embryo.

A powerful composition that brings a sense of urbanity to a suburban setting.

regions of car parks and rubbish disposal points. A double-pitch roof frames a large window that is emphasised by its copper-clad projection, glazed ground-floor corners suggest a continuity of space between inside and out, while a simple arcade seems to protect people, gather them and encourage them to move into the building. And the long roof stretches backwards, implying that there is a space beyond the immediate facade and the enclosures it unfolds. A few tables in the precinct, and one could imagine oneself in a small town in the French provinces, with an unusually successful *maire*. It certainly belies its setting on private land at the point where suburbs fade into green belt.

These are all appropriate impressions because this is a theatre, that architectural type which, after churches, has made illusion its stock-in-trade. Its architects are Arts Team @ RHWL who have designed almost as many theatres as Frank Matcham himself, and probably more if you include all those of Matcham's they have refurbished. But this is the first time these architects have completed one with school-level educational facilities combined. So wrapping around the simply planned main volume with foyer, auditorium, stage and backstage on axis, are ancillary spaces, one large enough to be used as a theatre studio or main teaching space, others adaptable for changing or seminar rooms, with one workshop. The foyer, double height with a balcony, makes a generous entrance space and is easily usable for extra teaching, meetings or exhibitions.

All this makes a nice adjacency diagram, but where the design really reveals its purpose is in the way it provides for teaching as well as practice of all aspects of theatre craft. For example, the control room can take a gaggle of girls and boys where a community or commercial theatre would have space for one technician. Similarly, the workshop functions almost as an art room as well as a production space. Web-like over the auditorium is a lighting grid, not only giving flexibility to lighting design but allowing potential lighting designers to gain practical experience in their trade. The 150 seats can be placed in numerous configurations – more, even, than a standard theatre that would not have the same easy access to free labour as a school. A gallery runs round the entire space, increasing the authenticity of productions and potentially allowing a simulation of Shakespearean theatre. Indeed, there is no stage or proscenium as such, merely wings and entrances to one end of the auditorium so that each production can have its own configuration. This is, as Arts Team partner Barry Pritchard says, a flexible instrument with which the school can experiment and expand its horizon.

Private schools like Chigwell are all engaged in a never-ending cycle of producing more, and better, facilities to justify the fees they charge, and charging higher fees to pay for them: the days when a blackboard, hard desk, unheated classroom, horsehair mattresses and cane-wielding masters in tatty mortarboards and torn degree gowns were enough are long gone. Then came the phase of excessive carpeting, central heating and food that made a shy at being edible – and that's no longer enough either. What facilities like Chigwell's drama centre represent is an interesting development, an architectural form which, however trendy the head of drama, still exudes a set of hierarchies between audience and performers, directors and cast, back- and front-of-house staff,

Top left
Seating about 150, the auditorium seats can fold back to make a flat floor, or to take a wide variety of stage configurations. A first-floor balcony runs around the space, and above is a lighting grid, as much for teaching as for flexibility of installation.

Top right
Distant view – a powerful form in a suburban setting.

Middle left
At night careful lighting enlivens the foyer and shows off features such as the strong wall that runs through the building, and the staircase to first-floor level.

Bottom left
The foyer is large enough for receptions, and doubles as a teaching space for drama classes.

but where each of these can invert the normal educational triangle of pupils, parents and teachers. Headmasters can tear tickets, junior students take leading roles and parents help behind the scenes. As such it has the potential to enrich an educational experience, just as those pre-Reformation monastic schools used to have annual festivals where, for one day, a junior boy would take the position of the abbot. *Pace* Lady Plowden, such experiences probably tell us all far more about ourselves than any amount of child-centred learning.

It also marks a significant point in the ongoing relationship between the institution and its architecture. Too many private schools last thought seriously about how to appoint an architect when they had to produce a war memorial. That was understandable half a century ago, but hardly likely still to cast a positive didactic spell. Theatre, with its origins in Western culture's most primeval practices, evokes a sense of magic, mystery and illusion. It offers ideal preparation for the future – when current pupils leave school and have to show interpersonal skills and flexibility in their approach to tasks, to command attention and present themselves – as well as reaching back into the depths of tradition. Grammar schools, themselves looking back to ancient Greece, made rhetoric an important part of their curriculum. At Chigwell, on a £1.9 million budget that precluded the temptation to overelaborate, Arts Team has shown how these ideas can be embodied in a bold but unfussy work of architecture, and demonstrated how a city-centre function like drama need not be out of place in a suburban setting. Δ+

Below
A chef at work in the Gund-Shapiro apartment. The kitchen was
built with shapes and materials that evoke the machine aesthetic,
according to a design by Markus Dochantschi, an associate of
Zaha Hadid.

Food Lab

At a time when most us domestic
design is flush and plush, **Craig Kellogg**
encounters, in the American kitchen,
a bracing opportunity for hard steel.
A kitchen renovation designed recently
by Markus Dochantschi, on the Upper
East Side of Manhattan, argues for
the revival of the machine aesthetic
in New York interiors.

When an automotive executive complained this year to
the *Wall Street Journal Europe* that some new cars had begun
to resemble 'angry kitchen appliances', he was flattering neither
the cars nor the world's appliance designers. Even as technology
for other rooms in American homes shrinks because of digital
miniaturisation, kitchens and kitchen machines have started
looking more muscular and overtly modern. In fact, it's perhaps
the American automotive industry's bloated sport-utility vehicles
that best mirror the current bigness in kitchens. By contrast,
fussy nostalgic elements like hand-trowelled plaster for kitchen
walls, or rustic Tuscan-tile floors, increasingly seem old-
fashioned and irrelevant.

Trendy futuristic cuisine – from the delectable foams being
whipped up by adventurous Spanish chefs, in association with
chemists, to fancy factory-processed frozen foods sold by
upscale supermarkets – suggest that we are less interested in
home cooking than ever before. But you wouldn't know that
from the time and attention we lavish on kitchen design. The

image that is cutting-edge today, somewhere between
food factory and science lab, makes sense in part
because kitchens have a history as functional rooms.
Architects once considered entire houses to be
'machines for living'. Now it's mostly kitchens that offer
a taste of the machine aesthetic in North American
residential architecture.

So why a hard, industrial look for residential kitchens
and not for our spotless bathrooms, with their matrix
plumbing pipes and ceramic tile walls? The traditional
bathroom ideals of sensuality and comfort mesh better
with soft Asian-inspired Minimalism than with the
bold, icy precision of the machine aesthetic.

Early associations between architecture and the
machine aesthetic date back to the dawn of the Modern
movement. The industrial design collection of New
York's Museum of Modern Art (MoMA), with its metal
implements taken directly from the factory floor, had

Top left
Halogen spotlights recessed in the ceiling illuminate the streamlined renovation.
Similar light fixtures have appeared in New York retail stores.

Top right
Dochantschi installed a floating island of wooden cabinetry,
with a cantilevering range hood hanging above. An appliance
alcove is notched into the casework of the rear wall.

Below
Machines such as a heavy-duty stand mixer by
Kitchen Aid are among small appliances in the
marketplace that express the machine aesthetic.

Left
Dochantschi's kitchen design incorporates a narrow,
space-saving, wood-panelled appliance alcove.

Top
Kitchen suppliers, such as casework prefabricator Boffi, support the trend towards Neomodernist kitchens. Functionalist elements and stainless-steel cabinetry contribute to the industrial aesthetic.

Bottom
A unit by Sub-Zero, the brand of Gund's refrigerator, took its cues from commercial models with glass doors.

untold influence in forming Modernist tastes. But it is worth remembering that silvery brushed metal once seemed as rare and titillating in architectural interiors as light-emitting diodes or eco-friendly coconut-wood floors are today.

On Manhattan's Park Avenue, the baronial art-filled apartment of noted collector Agnes Gund and her husband, Daniel Shapiro, is a mellow collage of styles. But Gund, a former president of MoMA, has built a crisply Modernist new kitchen. Gone are her 20-year-old linoleum counter tops, in favour of industrial stainless steel. 'You can have the hard edge in kitchens,' says her architect, Markus Dochantschi, a frequent collaborator with Zaha Hadid.

Although Gund is not someone who cooks seriously, she sought advice from a chef. Troupes of caterers visit often, and there can't be traffic jams. Dochantschi used animations to help Gund understand how traffic could flow. She opted for a freestanding central bench that seems not far removed from the factory floor. In a break with accepted ideas about kitchen finishes, some of the new cabinetry is flush white, in contrast to the rich mahogany panelling used for the base of the island and two walls of storage. The counter top is industrial stainless steel, for durability, and features a Le Cornue hob. 'People want to open the hood of a car and see the engine,' says Dochantschi. 'The first thing they touch in a kitchen is the stove.' An adjacent sink is for rinsing vegetables and filling pots with water. The sink for clean-up is part of a different traffic pattern.

The window, a rare jewel in any Manhattan kitchen, was reconfigured and enlarged to let in more light and fresh air. An armada of recessed adjustable spotlights has replaced the dated down-lights. But the gigantic side-by-side stainless-steel Sub-Zero refrigerator and freezer, along with double ovens, are recycled from the old kitchen.

The *New York Times* judged the new space 'ruthlessly efficient' but 'inviting'. Given that Gund's kitchen functions as an extension of her living room, it's not surprising to find space allotted to a table and adjacent book shelf. There is also art, in the form of a video that loops on the LCD flat-screen television mounted on the wall at the head of the table. At other times the monitor is used as a DVD player or a computer screen.

Dochantschi has started four more kitchens on the same scale and is also contributing to Hadid's American projects, including a new museum for Bartlesville. One architectural detail in Gund's kitchen is from the Rosenthal Center for Contemporary Art, the Hadid-designed museum in Cincinnati. The museum gift shop displays the same movable metal shelves. No surprise, Dochantschi worked on the design there, too. Δ+

Home Run:
Montreuil Housing

As part of a new series in Δ, Jane Briginshaw and Bruce Stewart profile new housing projects from around the world. In this first article, **Jane Briginshaw** describes an award-winning scheme by Paris-based office BNR, in Montreuil, just east of the city. She explains how, despite the limitations of a deep plan and restricted budget, the project has been able to deliver to council tenants homes that respond to their setting through 'a gentle green and bucolic landscape'.

'The typical low-rise Parisian suburb of Montreuil has its share of isolated towers.'
Because both sites were strongly marked by a topography of long thin strips, BNR was able to adapt the approach taken at Saintes to the project in Montreuil. In the 17th and 18th centuries Montreuil became famous for the cultivation of peaches. Deep and narrow plots, still very much in evidence today, created around the peach walls on the south-facing slopes developed into a very particular land use. As the town became denser deep paths to access the plot centres and blind gables characterising the detached houses joined

narrow building frontages. BNR set out to weave low-density housing into this urban fabric. The aim was to redescribe what they saw around them, recreating a dense occupation at ground-floor level, becoming less compact at first- and second-floor levels. They integrated new narrow paths, employed lightweight architecture to mirror garden sheds, kept the same setback as neighbouring houses and employed the same palette of colours.

Above
'BNR integrated new narrow paths, kept the same setback as neighbouring houses and employed the same palette of colours.'
The scheme is designed with an existing single house in its midst, even though the council had compulsory purchase powers. The architects welcomed any opportunities to mould the new scheme around the existing landscape. By placing rear gardens back to back, exploiting a layout familiar to British eyes, a gentle green and bucolic landscape results. Here in Montreuil the private gardens bleed into semi-public green spaces and dividing fences are deliberately left transparent to maintain views through the whole plot. The result is continuous green space with boundaries left uncertain, quite different from the regular and sharply defined UK back gardens. The entrance halls are light with views through to the gardens connecting the street frontage to the plot interiors. There are also extra garden areas, one used as a children's play area and another for barbecues, which seem to work well. An important and conscious decision has been made to favour collectivity over isolation, a positive approach resisting current pressures for us all to retreat into secure separation.

Opposite
'Within the plot interiors a gentle green and bucolic landscape results.'
Although the plan at ground-floor level formalises strategic choices it is not always successful. The problem of getting light into a deep plan is tackled by using internal patios, but because full glazing was unaffordable interiors do not benefit. The patios feel small and dark. The clients demanded that the flats were laid out traditionally and the spaces are not generous, even though the bathrooms are large. The fluidity that may have been created with open-plan kitchens or more glazing underplays the possibilities that BNR has worked hard to create. But this is the result of deliberate choices. The budget was restricted and some architects have refused equivalent commissions, arguing that the future occupants deserve more generously financed housing. But BNR took on the challenge, understanding that strategic decisions like adopting an expensive ground-floor layout with a long lineage of facade would result in compromises elsewhere.

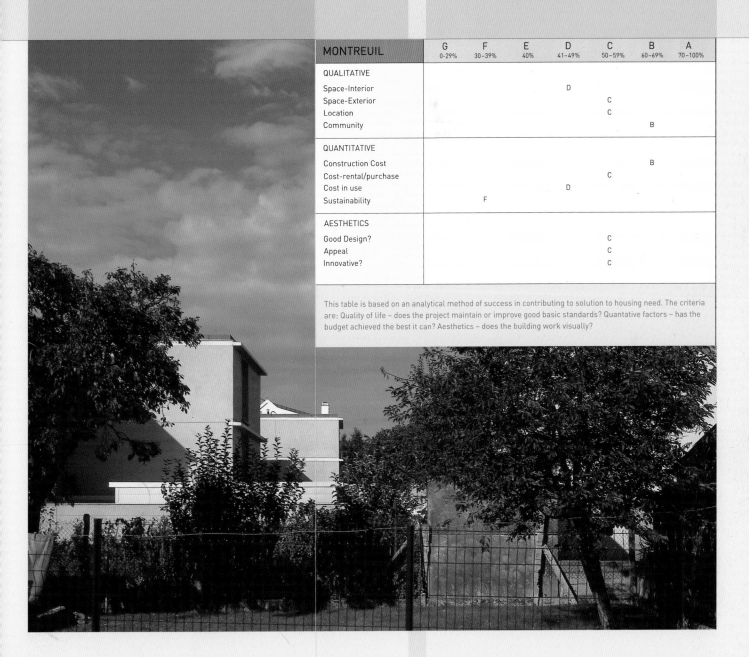

MONTREUIL	G 0-29%	F 30-39%	E 40%	D 41-49%	C 50-59%	B 60-69%	A 70-100%
QUALITATIVE							
Space-Interior				D			
Space-Exterior					C		
Location					C		
Community						B	
QUANTITATIVE							
Construction Cost						B	
Cost-rental/purchase					C		
Cost in use				D			
Sustainability		F					
AESTHETICS							
Good Design?					C		
Appeal					C		
Innovative?					C		

This table is based on an analytical method of success in contributing to solution to housing need. The criteria are: Quality of life – does the project maintain or improve good basic standards? Quantative factors – has the budget achieved the best it can? Aesthetics – does the building work visually?

It is not often that a young practice gets the opportunity to build a sizable social-housing scheme, let alone influence local planning. It was on the strength of winning the Europan competition in 1994 for a low-density housing project in Saintes, western France, that the freshly graduated partners of BNR (Thibaud Babled, Armand Nouvet and Marc Reynaud) were invited to enter a closed local-authority competition for 36 dwellings in Montreuil, on the eastern edge of Paris. The judges recognised that the young team proposed an architecture with a real affinity to Montreuil's urban landscape. This brought about not only a commission to build the project but also an invitation to help them revise local planning regulations. The resulting scheme won the prestigious Le Moniteur First Building prize in 2002. Thoughtful and sensitive, BNR's architecture draws attention away from itself, out towards its surroundings and in this it has been compared to the work of Sergison Bates and Tony Fretton.

Unlike London and cities in the UK, where the poorest housing stock is generally deemed to be in the city centres with tower blocks punctuating the inner cities, some of the wealthiest areas of Paris are concentrated in the middle of the city, with high-rise housing projects ringing the outskirts. It was only in the 1980s and 1990s that architects worldwide started to learn lessons in social housing from the acute problems created by these infamous 1960s *cités* of tower and slab blocks.

Architects began to understand that towers brutally implanted in traditional low-density suburbs created isolated islands, alienating neighbours and imprisoning inhabitants. Some also began to recognise that, within cities like Paris, the impact of residential towers could

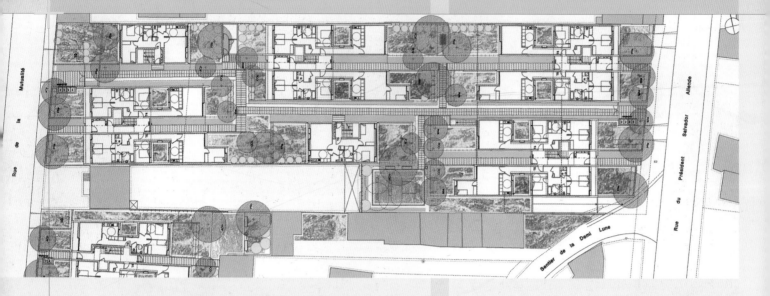

Above
'The problem of getting light into a deep plan is tackled by using internal patios.'
BNR had wanted a pyramid-like form for each block with a wide base breaking down
into balconies at the top level. However, this was not possible and the result is
reminiscent of Auguste Perret's reconstruction of Le Havre begun in 1945. Efforts
were made within the low budget: a specialist render finish was used on the outside
and PVC window frames are not the standard white, but these are not enough to
pull the materials out of the ordinary. Interestingly the similar project at Saintes,
on site at the moment, is transformed by using natural honey-coloured rough stone.

Right
'The architects have used a theoretical approach to imagine a low-density project.'
This approach mimics the existing fabric and becomes part of it without pastiche. The
considerable urban/architectural achievement gives the council tenants in their homes
the ability to integrate into their surroundings. Clear conceptual choices have led to
a scheme that is socially successful and the overall feel of the development is at the
same time intimate and spacious. Although the interior living spaces and materials are
unexceptional, BNR thoroughly deserved the prize for a first building. In giving priority
to a brief wider than the building-as-object, they have tackled the most important things
first. In the complex reality of producing architecture, this is a real accomplishment.

be accommodated. They saw that existing services could be
stretched to the new residents, or if new amenities were
necessary they could be shared, breaking down boundaries
between people.

Through trial and error a consensus has developed that the
urban environment should supply the starting point. This is
adopted as much by the neo-Corbusian school (architects like
Catherine Furet, the high priestess of classic French Modernist
housing, featured in the forthcoming issue of △) as by BNR.
The difference is further down the line in the articulation of
site and form, BNR believing that space is not necessarily
the primary consideration. The projects are generated from
a diligent site analysis and immersion in the building's context.
The solutions extend beyond the building form back into the
surroundings, playing down the forms themselves and making
them subsidiary, by merging or reflecting, the responses
blurring the differences between new and old. △+

Note
In Montreuil a remarkable reordering came about that may have a wider influence
on future developments than the project itself. Considering its own heritage, the
local council of Montreuil, while embarking on its once-in-a-generation review
of the planning process, determined to think more widely than usual. Knowing
that traditional planning regulations based on universal abstract ideas seemed
to deliver the same sort of projects that were relatively unresponsive to the local
environment, the mayor decided to change direction. He proposed that the POS
(Plan d'occupation du sol) should be replaced by a morphological plan, and he
invited architects working on local projects (Alvaro Siza and BNR amongst them)
to propose new rules. This led to a much more specific set of regulations tailored
to the local urban environment that will systematise the integrated and responsive
urban approach favoured by BNR and others.

Jane Briginshaw and Bruce Stewart are currently researching and writing
The Architects' Navigation Guide to New Housing, to be published in autumn
2005 by Wiley-Academy.
    Jane Briginshaw is a practising architect and architectural design lecturer
at the University of Greenwich, London. She was a local council speaker on
housing and a candidate in the 2004 European elections.
    Bruce Stewart has practised as an architect and is currently lecturing in
architectural design at the University of Greenwich, and architectural history
and theory at the Bartlett School of Architecture.

Left and bottom left
National Glass Centre, Sunderland, 1994
The glass centre is a public facility with glass-production studios coexisting in a close relationship, demonstrating that the industry is still going strong. Set on a sloping site on the edge of the banks of the Wear, the centre responds to its context. The ground was carved out to accommodate the expressed steel-framed structure. Creating an innovative building typology that compresses the scheme's disparate functions within one envelope, the practice explores the possibilities of them sitting side by side. A working factory coexists with a series of independent workshops for smaller-scale designer-glass production, gallery spaces, a café, restaurant and other public facilities, set in a double-height space under one glazed roof.

GolliferLangston
Architects

The British government has promised to change the face of education with a pledge from Gordon Brown in the 2004 spring budget to refurbish every school by 2015. **Lucy Bullivant** profiles a practice that has immersed itself in educational ideas since winning a scheme for the National Glass Centre in Sunderland. Here she takes a look at Gollifer Langston Architects' completed museum, and pioneering designs for two city learning centres in London.

Langston Architects**Gollifer Langston** Architects**Gollifer Langston** Architects**Gollifer Langston** Architects**Gollifer Langston** Architects**Gollifer Langston** Architects**Gollifer Langston** Architects**Gollifer Langston** Architects**Gollifer Langston** Architects**Gollifer Langston** Architects**Gollifer Langston** Archite
itects**Gollifer Langston** Architects**Gollifer Langston** Architects**Gollifer Langston** Architects**Gollifer Langston** Architects**Gollifer Langston** Architects**Gollifer Langston** Architects**Gollifer Langston** Architects**Gollifer Langston** Architects**Gollifer Langston** Architects**Gollifer Langston** Archite
*Langston Architects**Gollifer Langston** Architects**Gollifer Langston** Architects**Gollifer Langston** Architects**Gollifer Langston** Architects**Gollifer Langston** Architects**Gollifer Langston** Architects**Gollifer Langston** Architects**Gollifer Langston** Architects**Gollifer Langston** Architects**Gollifer La
itects**Gollifer Langston** Architects**Gollifer Langston** Architects**Gollifer Langston** Architects**Gollifer Langston** Architects**Gollifer Langston** Architects**Gollifer Langston** Architects**Gollifer Langston** Architects**Gollifer Langston** Architects**Gollifer Langston** Architects**Gollifer Langston** Archite
*Langston Architects**Gollifer Langston** Architects**Gollifer Langston** Architects**Gollifer Langston** Architects**Gollifer Langston** Architects**Gollifer Langston** Architects**Gollifer Langston** Architects**Gollifer Langston** Architects**Gollifer Langston** Architects**Gollifer Langston** Architects**Gollifer La
itects**Gollifer Langston** Architects**Gollifer Langston** Architects**Gollifer Langston** Architects**Gollifer Langston** Architects**Gollifer Langston** Architects**Gollifer Langston** Architects**Gollifer Langston** Architects**Gollifer Langston** Architects**Gollifer Langston** Architects**GolliferLa

Social and technological changes have impacted upon the act of formal learning at all levels. Fresh typological interpretations by architects have been slow in coming, but the work of practices like Gollifer Langston, who are reinventing space in this field, represents a huge cultural investment in the changes that are taking place towards a greater accessibility of resources. The accolade of Millennium Product status was recently bestowed on the firm's first building, a simple and innovative solution for the award-winning National Glass Centre in Sunderland, and its new schemes for a number of inner-city learning centres look set to widely influence future examples.

City learning centres have undergone a thorough process of rethinking their educational role. Visiting the first two completed centres by Gollifer Langston, one evident hallmark of the architects' approach is their pragmatism and modest attention to detail. However, it is their flair for mixing spatial arrangements transparently and nonhierarchically, matching a new proximity of functions, that distinguishes them from many practices. 'We've been lucky as most of our projects have been for clients who decided they wanted to break the mould,' explains Andy Gollifer, codirector, with Mark Langston, of the practice.

In practice now for 10 years, the architects know their field extremely well at the levels of theory and practice. Gollifer, who studied under architect John Miller at the Royal College of Art in the 1980s, sees the pitfalls of architectural language if addressing social change is the objective. He talks about 'polite Modernism' that 'is too polite. In architecture you have to be able to work on all levels. It needs to be pragmatic and spontaneous, calm and shouting at the same time, because life is that complicated.'

Gollifer Langston was under a year old when the practice won a major competition for the National Glass Centre in Sunderland in 1994. Two years later, once the funding was in place, it started on site. The result catapulted the firm into the headlines, and although highly successful its profile has been relatively low since then, time which has been spent building on its skills after this grand entry into construction. Initiated by the Tyne and Wear development corporation, part funded by the European Regional Development Fund (ERDF), and made possible through a grant from the Lottery, the £7.5 million building was completed in 1998.

ArchitectsGolliferLangstonArchitectsGolliferLangstonArchitectsGolliferLangstonArchitectsGolliferLangstonArchitectsGolliferLangstonArchitectsGolliferLangstonArchitectsGolliferLangstonArchitectsGolliferLangstonArchitectsGolliferLangstonArchitectsGolliferLangstonArchitectsGolliferLangstonArchitectsGollifer
liferLangstonArchitectsGolliferLangstonArchitectsGolliferLangstonArchitectsGolliferLangstonArchitectsGolliferLangstonArchitectsGolliferLangstonArchitectsGolliferLangstonArchitectsGolliferLangstonArchitectsGolliferLangstonArchitectsGolliferLangstonArchitectsGolliferLangstonArc
ArchitectsGolliferLangstonArchitectsGolliferLangstonArchitectsGolliferLangstonArchitectsGolliferLangstonArchitectsGolliferLangstonArchitectsGolliferLangstonArchitectsGolliferLangstonArchitectsGolliferLangstonArchitectsGolliferLangstonArchitectsGolliferLangstonArchitectsGollifer
liferLangstonArchitectsGolliferLangstonArchitectsGolliferLangstonArchitectsGolliferLangstonArchitectsGolliferLangstonArchitectsGolliferLangstonArchitectsGolliferLangstonArchitectsGolliferLangstonArchitectsGolliferLangstonArchitectsGolliferLangstonArchitectsGolliferLangstonArc
ArchitectsGolliferLangstonArchitectsGolliferLangstonArchitectsGolliferLangstonArchitectsGolliferLangstonArchitectsGolliferLangstonArchitectsGolliferLangstonArchitectsGolliferLangstonArchitectsGolliferLangstonArchitectsGolliferLangstonArchitectsGolliferLangstonArchitectsGollifer
liferLangstonArchitectsGolliferLangstonArchitectsGolliferLangstonArchitectsGolliferLangstonArchitectsGolliferLangstonArchitectsGolliferLangstonArchitectsGolliferLangstonArchitectsGolliferLangstonArchitectsGolliferLangstonArchitectsGolliferLangstonArchitectsGolliferLangstonArc

National Glass Centre, Sunderland
Opposite
The facade is glass hung from the front columns, which also support the front walkways and shading, and was designed with Arup, who also designed the glass roof. All the public elements are positioned close to the river, so visitors can look back into the workshops and out from wherever they are in what feels like a covered walkway. The ambience of the centre is of a factory, not a shed, but one with a public face – a rare combination of functions that provides a dynamic and stimulating atmosphere.

● ● ● ● ● ● ●

King's Cross City Learning Centre, London, 2003
Above
Together with the South Camden CLC, the centre at King's Cross demonstrates how a transparent and nonhierarchical spatial arrangement matches a new proximity of educational functions. Initiated by the Department for Education and Skills (DfES), the two centres serve as a bench mark for future CLC development. The King's Cross CLC building opens up on its public side with a new forecourt shaded by two existing plane trees providing solar shading. Its facilities are organised around a double-height space that can be accessed from the school behind. Clad in fibre cement panels and curtain-wall glazing with black lignacite blocks inside, the building is a simple form, and this solution serves to emphasise transparency at night.

Set on a disused area on the edge of the banks of the Wear, the centre responds to its context with an expressed steel-framed structure set on a sloping site, carved out to create the whole area. It is a building with an innovative and complex building typology that the practice is clearly at ease designing. 'It compresses all its disparate functions within one envelope and explores the possibilities of them sitting side by side. It was much more interesting to combine public and work spaces,' explains Gollifer. 'The point was to say: We've lost all the traditional industries, but glass production is still going strong, and here is its symbolic heart under one roof. We tried to get the transparency in.' So a working factory coexists with a series of independent workshops for smaller-scale designer-glass production, a café, restaurant, foyer and other public facilities on the ground floor, and gallery spaces, a seminar pod and upper foyer on the upper floor connected by a ramp and set in a double-height space under one glazed roof.

The relationship between structure, facade and river is very clean: the facade is glass, hung from the front columns, which also support the front walkways and

LangstonArchitectsGolliferLangstonArchitectsGolliferLangstonArchitectsGolliferLangstonArchitectsGolliferLangstonArchitectsGolliferLangstonArchitectsGolliferLangstonArchitectsGolliferLangstonArchitectsGolliferLangstonArchitectsGolliferLangstonArchitectsGolliferLangstonArchite
hitectsGolliferLangstonArchitectsGolliferLangstonArchitectsGolliferLangstonArchitectsGolliferLangstonArchitectsGolliferLangstonArchitectsGolliferLangstonArchitectsGolliferLangstonArchitectsGolliferLangstonArchitectsGolliferLangstonArchitectsGolliferLangstonArchitectsGolliferLangstonArchite
hitectsGolliferLangstonArchitectsGolliferLangstonArchitectsGolliferLangstonArchitectsGolliferLangstonArchitectsGolliferLangstonArchitectsGolliferLangstonArchitectsGolliferLangstonArchitectsGolliferLangstonArchitectsGolliferLangstonArchitectsGolliferLangstonArchitectsGolliferLa
Langston Architects GolliferLangston Architects GolliferLangston Architects GolliferLangston Architects GolliferLangston Architects GolliferLangston Architects GolliferLangston Architects GolliferLangston Architects GolliferLangston Architects GolliferLangston Archite
hitectsGolliferLangstonArchitectsGolliferLangstonArchitectsGolliferLangstonArchitectsGolliferLangstonArchitectsGolliferLangstonArchitectsGolliferLangstonArchitectsGolliferLangstonArchitectsGolliferLangstonArchitectsGolliferLangstonArchitectsGolliferLa

King's Cross City Learning Centre
Above
Visualisation of the building's street elevation. To add to its presence, digital 'manifestation' dots on the glazing form letters announcing the building's purpose. Gollifer Langston believes that 'detail must enhance the constructional nature of a building'. Adding to the language of materials is a crèche (to the left of the entrance) made in corrugated polycarbonate.

Left
The open ambience of the double-height space. The space functions as a reception and open-plan learning area with computers and mobile furniture, but also includes a recording studio. The library and classrooms are on the floor above, the library visually accessible through glazed panels. This juxtaposition allows the perception of different things happening side by side. The two floors are closely physically linked and wrapped around the lightwell over the reception desk painted bright orange and visible from the garden. The architects use exposed concrete rather than suspended ceilings, preferring the rawness and unfinished quality of industrial materials. They also include hanging Snowcrash suspended panels with a felt finish that even out the live acoustics resulting from the open-plan space.

South Camden City Learning Centre, London, 2001
Opposite
A newbuild scheme next to an existing school, South Camden provides facilities for IT, design and multimedia for use by primary and secondary schools as well as local community members, and dining facilities in a large hall. The new building is set up from its street elevation, a massively long structure that twists the facade, which is punctured with circular holes and includes a double-height glazed common entrance. By giving the centre this kind of distinctive public facade the architects set the scene for new technology-based learning and its collaborative, interactive methods. The ground-floor spaces are styled like a bar of a restaurant, connected to one another, and linked via an open metal staircase to more self-contained learning areas on the floor above.

ArchitectsGolliferLangstonArchitectsGolliferLangstonArchitectsGolliferLangstonArchitectsGolliferLangstonArchitectsGolliferLangstonArchitectsGolliferLangstonArchitectsGolliferLangstonArchitectsGolliferLangstonArchitectsGolliferLangstonArchitectsGollifer
liferLangstonArchitectsGolliferLangstonArchitectsGolliferLangstonArchitectsGolliferLangstonArchitectsGolliferLangstonArchitectsGolliferLangstonArchitectsGolliferLangstonArchitectsGolliferLangstonArchitectsGolliferLangstonArchitectsGolliferLangstonArc
ArchitectsGolliferLangstonArchitectsGolliferLangstonArchitectsGolliferLangstonArchitectsGolliferLangstonArchitectsGolliferLangstonArchitectsGolliferLangstonArchitectsGolliferLangstonArchitectsGolliferLangstonArchitectsGolliferLangstonArchitectsGollifer
liferLangstonArchitectsGolliferLangstonArchitectsGolliferLangstonArchitectsGolliferLangstonArchitectsGolliferLangstonArchitectsGolliferLangstonArchitectsGolliferLangstonArchitectsGolliferLangstonArchitectsGolliferLangstonArchitectsGolliferLangstonArc
ArchitectsGolliferLangstonArchitectsGolliferLangstonArchitectsGolliferLangstonArchitectsGolliferLangstonArchitectsGolliferLangstonArchitectsGolliferLangstonArchitectsGolliferLangstonArchitectsGolliferLangstonArchitectsGolliferLangstonArchitectsGollifer
liferLangstonArchitectsGolliferLangstonArchitectsGolliferLangstonArchitectsGolliferLangstonArchitectsGolliferLangstonArchitectsGolliferLangstonArchitectsGolliferLangstonArchitectsGolliferLangstonArchitectsGolliferLangstonArchitectsGolliferLangstonArc

shading. Designed with Arup, along with the glazed roof, the facade gives a high degree of openness to the view and all of the public elements are positioned close to the river so that visitors can look back into the workshops and out from wherever they are in what feels like a covered walkway.

Battle McCarthy designed the natural ventilation towers and earth tube for natural cooling and heat recycling from factory to public areas. Although the glass centre is an industrial building and as such a big container, the building's character is that of a factory, not a shed. 'Shed' implies something that makes little concession to where it sits, whereas the centre is very site-specific, 'seeking to give a new sense of place to a lost piece of riverside'.

King's Cross and South Camden city learning centres are two of a second wave of city learning centres (CLCs) initiated by the Department for Education and Skills (DfES). Designed by the practice the centres, in north London, contribute the necessary architectural vision these hybrid facilities need. Given that the DfES plans to build 30 CLCs in inner-city areas around the country, Gollifer Langston's designs serve as a bench mark. As centres devoted to language learning, the CLCs are designed as a physical focus to create a local community in which a wealth of different languages are understood, and incorporate the latest computer and communications technology, creating a link with other schools and bodies.

A vital theme Gollifer Langston has spatialised with great skill in both projects is that technology has radically changed the face of schools, and this has a direct impact on how space is used and what type of spaces are needed, to say

nothing of ventilation requirements and suitability of materials used. 'The reinvention comes from the brief,' say the architects.

While King's Cross was a newbuild scheme next to an existing school, South Camden was an entire site of buildings including those from the 1970s and 1980s, in an area where much regeneration is being carried out. The existing facilities were fragmented, and the architects wanted to 'reinforce the context' and create a sense of security and connection. First they undertook the development planning work. 'Looking at the whole, it was a question of identifying where the difficulties were and then knitting the spaces back together. There was a fear on the client side of a grand statement being imposed.' Sometimes it is not a question of building, but making connections, master-planning on a medium scale, says Gollifer.

The practice's role was to respond to changing needs (numbers attending, demographics and curriculum) and extended to raising funding for the new building the firm was to create, with facilities for IT, design and multimedia for use by primary and secondary schools as well as local community members, and dining facilities in a large hall.

The need for flexibility and informality of working and more collaborative, interactive learning methods are addressed in ground-floor educational spaces styled like a bar of a restaurant and linked by a metal staircase to more self-contained work areas upstairs.

Langston Architects **Gollifer** Langston Architects **Gollifer** Langston Architects **Gollifer** Langston Architects **Gollifer** Langston Architects **Gollifer** Langston Architects **Gollifer** Langston Architects **Gollifer** Langston Architects **Gollifer** Langston Architects **Gollifer** Langston Architects **Gollifer** Langston Architect
Langston Architects **Gollifer** Langston Architects **Gollifer** Langston Architects **Gollifer** Langston Architects **Gollifer** Langston Architects **Gollifer** Langston Architects **Gollifer** Langston Architects **Gollifer** Langston Architects **Gollifer** Langston Architects **Gollifer** Langston Architects **Gollifer** Langston Architects **Gollifer** Langston Archite
hitects **Gollifer** Langston Architects **Gollifer** Langston Architects **Gollifer** Langston Architects **Gollifer** Langston Architects **Gollifer** Langston Architects **Gollifer** Langston Architects **Gollifer** Langston Architects **Gollifer** Langston Architects **Gollifer** Langston Architects **Gollifer** Langston Architects **Gollifer** Langston Archite
Langston Architects **Gollifer** Langston Architects **Gollifer** Langston Architects **Gollifer** Langston Architects **Gollifer** Langston Architects **Gollifer** Langston Architects **Gollifer** Langston Architects **Gollifer** Langston Architects **Gollifer** Langston Architects **Gollifer** Langston Architects **Gollifer** Langston Architects **Gollifer** Langston Archit
hitects **Gollifer** Langston Architects **Gollifer** Langston Architects **Gollifer** Langston Architects **Gollifer** Langston Architects **Gollifer** Langston Architects **Gollifer** Langston Architects **Gollifer** Langston Architects **Gollifer** Langston Architects **Gollifer** Langston Architects **Gollifer** Langston Architects **Gollifer** Langston Archite
hitects **Gollifer** Langston Architects **Gollifer** Langston Architects **Gollifer** Langston Architects **Gollifer** Langston Architects **Gollifer** Langston Architects **Gollifer** Langston Architects **Gollifer** Langston Architects **Gollifer** Langston Architects **Gollifer** Langston Architects **Gollifer** Langston Architects **Gollifer** Langston Architects **GolliferLar**

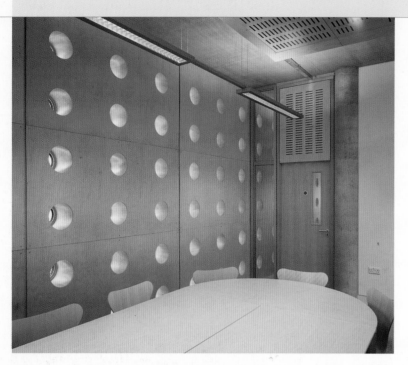

South Camden City Learning Centre
Left
On the first floor, the hole punctures also appear in some of the meeting-room walls, making them seem like screens, a device that connects street and working space.

601fx, Dean Street, Soho, London, 1996
Opposite
601fx is a film company specialising in computer-generated special effects, and here the practice dealt with space in response to new creative uses, allowing the views between different activities to open up. As with changes in music, the technology for producing film has changed, making a light and bright environment acceptable. This freedom is exploited for transparency, in the space and through the facade, with perforated metal panels that control light and become translucent, and mirrors to increase the appearance of depth. Instead of partitions, a series of screens defines space by subtle environmental change.

Yet the same contemporary accessibility as well as use of industrial materials is built into the design as at King's Cross.

The new building is set up from its street elevation, a massively long structure that twists the facade with a common entrance point that is punctured with holes. As a result light comes in but the views out are limited. 'It's an inward-looking space. It's nice to have a slightly glimpsed view of the outside.' This technique appears in some of the meeting-room walls, a device that connects street and working space.

The King's Cross CLC building opens up on its public side with a new forecourt shaded by two existing plane trees providing solar shading. Its facilities are organised around a double-height space that can be accessed from the school behind. This area functions as a reception and open-plan learning area with computers and mobile furniture, but also includes a recording studio. The more contemplative areas of the library and classrooms are on the floor above, the library visually accessible through glazed panels. This juxtaposition 'makes for a much more dynamic feeling to the space,' says Gollifer. 'It's important to enjoy different things happening side by side.' Material interventions that show discrimination include a library resources 'box' with a glass window in bright green Lensvelt solid-core laminate. The two floors are physically closely linked and wrapped around the lightwell over the reception desk, which is painted bright orange and visible from the garden.

Clad in fibre cement panels and curtain-wall glazing with black Lignacite blocks inside, the building is a simple form, a solution that serves to emphasise transparency at night. A glass shelter above the entrance, with a cantilevered steel frame to emphasise it, echoes the language of the glass centre, itself a big steel frame. Adding to the language of materials is a crèche to the left of the entrance made in corrugated polycarbonate.

To add to the building's presence, digital 'manifestation' dots on the glazing form letters announcing the building's purpose. Gollifer Langston believes that 'detail must enhance the constructional nature of a building'. But this is but one facet of a coherent whole, and both CLCs have what the architects define as an environmental strategy. This includes exposed concrete rather than suspended ceilings. 'We enjoy the rawness and unfinished quality of industrial materials.' An interesting feature is the Snowcrash acoustic panels suspended from the ceiling with a felt finish, which counteract the live acoustics such an open-plan arrangement brings. This is a friendly and accessible building where openness is conveyed in a fairly expressive manner: 'Things don't necessarily have to be closed in.'

The practice is currently designing an extension to house performing-arts teaching and activities at Acland Burghley School, also in Camden, a concrete slab building by HKPA that Gollifer feels might be a Brutalist milestone, but one he is is prepared to deal with. Learning architecture at Bristol University, 'everyone was force-fed Corb, and his ideas were a kind of gospel in those days, but the positive aspect stays with you'. The practice draws on his 'real rigour', simplicity, the focus on 'the architect's route through the building that's inherent, guided by colours and walls', and treatments of space without flat walls. In the recording studio at King's Cross CLC they break up the typical regularity of that typology, and Gollifer refers to a precedent, the ground-breaking Metropolis, a suite of recording studios designed by Powell-Tuck Connor and Orefelt in the late 1980s that he oversaw as project architect. Just as the performance and recording of music has changed, a new architecture is needed to house these activities. The mixing desk becomes the centre of operations, and studios have access to daylight, both features of the firm's music centre at King's Cross and the scheme for Acland Burghley.

The practice's scheme for 601fx, a film company specialising in computer-generated special effects, in Dean Street, Soho, in central London, close to the

ArchitectsGolliferLangstonArch

architects' office, deals with space in response to new creative uses in a similar way to Metropolis. 'It allows the views between different activities to open up. As with changes in music, the technology for producing film has changed so it's no longer in a darkened room using a 21-inch monitor.' Instead the environment is light and bright, a boon allowing staff engaged most of the time in the environment of the computer monitor to focus on the middle distance. Here the architects exploit the facade with perforated metal panels that control light and become translucent, and mirrors to increase the appearance of depth. 'They become like a series of screens,' Gollifer explains. 'It's about what you reveal or not. When you take things out of boxes, you have to think of other ways to define space by subtle change.

'We are quite European in being unselfconscious about the materials we use. We live and work in a culture where things have to be dressed, coated and finely tuned. Buildings become weighed down or overwrought. There's a need for refreshingly resolved solutions, and a different kind of respect for context.' Both Gollifer and Langston believe they have found 'their language from their circumstances'. They have worked almost exclusively with 'newer institutions' and on schemes like recording studios in a period characterised by a wave of change. 'More, and different, functions are coming in – things that have not previously felt so accessible to people – and are blurring the boundaries.'

'It's a bit of a contemporary obsession that everything should be accessible,' Gollifer adds, this politically correct buzzword covering everything from the Internet to New Labour's policies for education and health centres, to drive-in McDonald's and reality TV. All the more reason for Corbusier's idea that the building can actually guide to maintain its currency in this cultural environment. Gollifer cites Superstudio's 'endless plateau' as a good metaphor for an accessible place that is nowhere, and can be anything from a family house to a picnic space. The opposite is a subtly controlled place, where you are guided by everything. In the glass centre, the practice clearly tries to hold on to the latter to help people appreciate it, but likewise, in its openness, the plateau concept also plays a role. The architects take the plateau and put a hole in it, and put a ramp in to take you somewhere. If a building like King's Cross promises free access for a multitude of functions, its architecture 'should have the same spirit; we are giving public access to a process'.

Lucy Bullivant is an architectural critic, author and curator. She has curated many exhibitions and symposia including 'Space Invaders: New UK Architecture' (British Council, 2001), Archis magazine's London events series (1998–01) and '4dspace' (ICA, 2003). She contributes to a number of international publications including Architectural Record, Domus and Archis. She was also the guest-editor of Home Front: New Developments in Housing, the July/August 2003 issue of ᴁ, and is writing a new book on the younger generation of UK architects for Thames & Hudson.

GolliferLangston
Architects

Resumé

1994	Gollifer Langston Architects established
	National Glass Centre Competition win
1996	Soho 601 project completed (two sites, 601 and 601fx)
1997	Development plans commissioned for Camden schools
1998	National Glass Centre, Sunderland, completed
1999	Bowes Museum Design competition for Northern Arts/Bowes Museum
	Ally Capellino shop and HQ completed
2000	Proposals for Newcastle Guildhall
2001	South Camden CLC completed
2002	Classrooms of the Future proposal
	Broadwater Farm campus proposal
	City and Islington College projects commence design
2003	Acland Burghley Performing Arts Building commences design
	King's Cross CLC: platform 1 completed
	Brentford CLC and Recording Studio starts on site Δ+

Top
The 'analog computing' form-finding process commences with the definition of networks using wetted yarn.

Bottom
Detail from drawing of nested cutting paths for CNC fabrication of structural ribs.

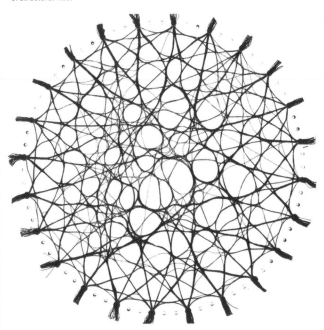

Whereas many of the generation of architects who have embraced digital techniques in their work have done so unreservedly, others favour a hybrid approach that deploys the computer only where it is most effective. The work of Lars Spuybroek and his NOX studio falls into this latter category, and in the following case study in the 'Blurring the Lines' series, **André Chaszar** describes the design and fabrication processes on one of these architects' current projects, in which digital and analog processes are closely intertwined – both potentially contributing to emergent behaviour.

Blurring the Lines:
An Exploration of Current CAD/CAM Techniques

Son-O-House

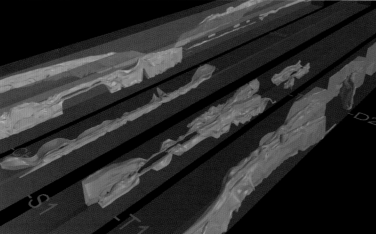

Top left
The analog computing process continues with bent/twisted
paper models of pathways at a more detailed scale.

Top right
Analog computing at the planning scale concludes with the
definition of pavilion volumes with additions to the paper model.

Bottom left
Digital modelling studies of pathways.

Bottom right
Digital rendering for visualisation and presentation purposes
of pavilion volumes including constructional elements.

Opposite, top left
Structural engineers' digital analysis model displaying
sense and magnitude of bending movements in the
pavilion's various rib elements.

Opposite, top right
The detailed design of the skin system begins with
curvature analysis of the pavilion surfaces.

Opposite, bottom
Part of the vector drawing file generated from the
digital model of the pavilion showing arrangement
of ribs, profiles and joints.

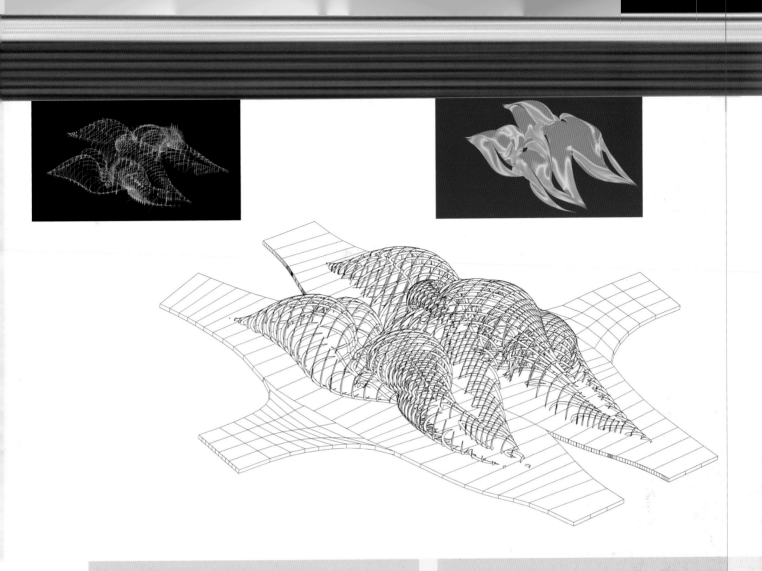

Son-O-House, NOX studio's current project for a sculptural pavilion structure with interactive sonic components, is an occupiable recreational and educational space in Son en Breugel, the Netherlands. The project comprises rather amorphous, very complex forms, and in our ongoing exploration of digital design and fabrication techniques in contemporary architecture it is instructive to see how the architects have integrated their use of the computer within an otherwise highly craft-oriented approach. This approach has many aspects that are now being discussed under the rubric of 'emergence', and it is interesting on the one hand to compare the kinds of emergent behaviours displayed in NOX's analog processes with those sought by advocates of digital methods, and on the other to see how the digital and analog processes interweave along the path of the projects' trajectories from the fluid conceptual to the specific instrumental, and finally physically real stages.

The Son-O-House project's grounding in paths of movement by visitors through the pavilion led to some initial formal studies carried out with the aid of moistened yarn stretched crosswise on a circular frame. The individual strands of yarn dispersed due to immersion and rejoined in new patterns upon drying. Path-like shapes suggested by these studies were then modelled by the architects using strips of paper slitted and twisted into various configurations. Further development of this concept resulted in the gradual definition of spatial volumes generated in a subsequent model by sets of parallel paper strips bent perpendicularly over and through the 'path' strips. In each of these stages of modelling the forms resulted, to a large extent, from the reaction of the materials used to physical forces (bending, twisting, surface tension, etc) in a complex, only partially predictable fashion.

These processes can be understood as a form of 'analog computing' reminiscent of some 19th- and 20th-century engineering 'form-finding' studies (such as those by Gaudí, Otto and so on) though, of course, with the significant difference that the NOX studies are not aimed in any way at mimicking or analysing and improving structural load-bearing behaviour. In this sense they are very similar to – and in fact, arguably, direct substitutes for – the digital form-finding exercises currently undertaken by many avant-garde architects who rely instead on shearing, torquing, mapping and other more exotic deformational algorithms built into the various modelling software packages at their disposal. To be sure, there is a not insignificant degree of authorial intervention present

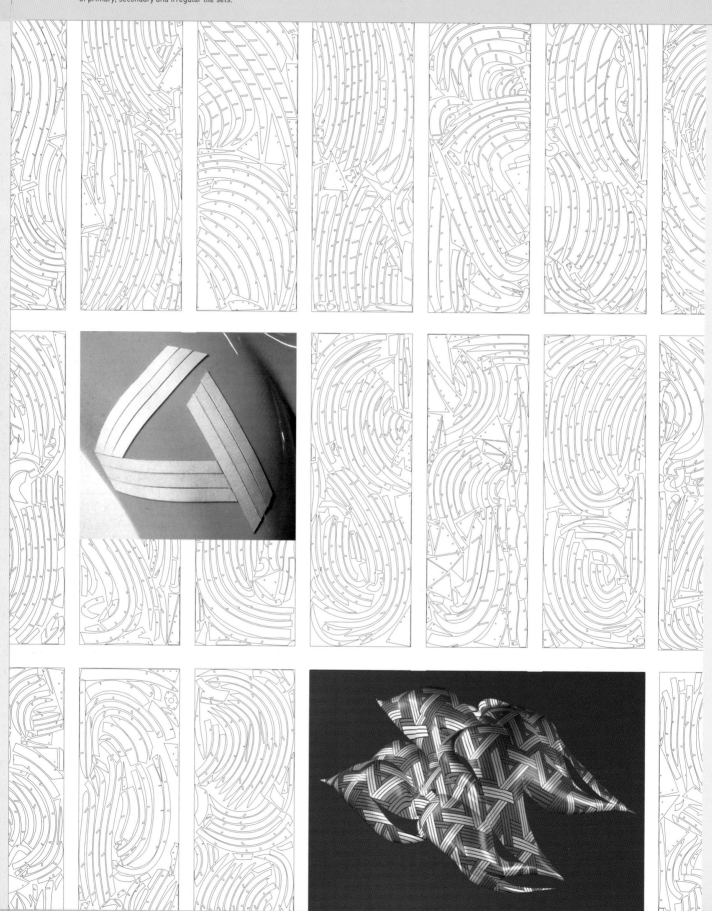

Below left
Skin detailing continues with physical studies of tiling schemes – another, simpler example of analog computing.

Below right
The tiling scheme mapped on to the digital model of the pavilion volumes showing areas of primary, secondary and irregular tile sets.

Background
Part of the nested layout of 2-D digital rib profiles generated from a 3-D digital model and manipulated to allow subdivision of profiles where necessary to reduce material wastage.

Below left
Construction photo of the pavilion framing and skin nearing completion.

Below right
Interior view of the completed pavilion framing and skin.

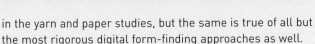

in the yarn and paper studies, but the same is true of all but the most rigorous digital form-finding approaches as well.

The digital component of NOX's work on the Son-O-House began during the paper-modelling stages with studies relating to the movement paths, and returned in greater extent as the designers began to grapple with issues of how to construct the pavilion. Collaboration with their engineers led to structuring the complex surfaces as a series of intersecting ribs that would support the outer skin. Digital modelling was integral to this stage of the work, first for definition of the rib profiles by sectioning of the pavilion forms, second for transmission of these rib locations and profiles to the structural engineers, and finally for computer-aided analysis of the forces and stresses in the resulting complex framework. The rib profiles were partially constrained by architectural considerations – particularly vis-à-vis the location of the outer pavilion surface and overlapping portions of this surface – so the engineering analysis was more focused on confirming rib spacings, thicknesses and material strengths than on shaping the ribs, as might also have been undertaken.

Design of a strategy for cladding the pavilion also relied in a mixed-mode fashion on digital as well as analog techniques. Curvature analysis of the digital model could do little more than confirm that significant portions of the surface were doubly curved and, thus, difficult to sheathe. Paper strips came into play again through a series of studies aimed at understanding how a set of identical flat elements could be arranged so as to 'tile' a doubly curved surface. It was proposed that by forming roughly triangular groupings of strips in a fashion akin to basket weaving (though without the overlapping), a large portion of the complex pavilion surface could be covered, with relatively little remaining to be clad by a combination of similar, smaller strips and finally of odd, uniquely shaped pieces. Although this process can be approximated in a digital model, it was far more quickly and flexibly explored by the simple expedient of the paper model, though tolerances of fitting the strips could not, of

course, be ensured by this means. Incidentally, the designers' application of such a cladding strategy meant that no digital cutting techniques were required, strictly speaking, for production of these elements.

However, fabrication of the framing ribs did require CNC cutting, due to the fact that there was no repetition whatsoever in the shapes and sizes of the ribs. Drawings produced from the digital model clearly convey the nature and complexity of the ribs and their joints, if not the system and sequence for assembling them. Efficient use of material for these oddly shaped elements required processing them into a rationalised layout, a function commonly performed by the 'nesting' routines in the software used to drive most CNC cutters. Significantly (and characteristically), however, the design team found that they could obtain better results – measured in terms of material use, if not in designers' time – through a semimanual process where the individual rib profiles were manipulated graphically according to more or less intuitive impulses. The reason for this was that whereas the programmed nesting routines would work with the ribs only as whole elements, a human designer could recognise instances where a rib could simply be cut so as to better fit on two adjacent sheets of material and later be spliced. Therefore, digital representations of the project's components, valued for their precision and ability to capture and convey detailed information, proved still more useful when augmented by a sort of 'analog' thought process that artificial intelligence development efforts are as yet only striving towards. Δ+

André Chaszar is a contributing editor of AD and a consulting engineer with an independent practice in New York. This article is the second in a series of case studies that illustrate the concepts and techniques of CAD/CAM in contemporary architecture, which were first introduced in the initial 'Blurring the Lines' series that appeared in the 2003 volume of *Architectural Design*. These and other texts will be collected in a book of the same title to be published by Wiley-Academy in early 2005.

Below
View of the ceremonial reception hall at night. Onyx walls, thin enough to allow light to penetrate, create a glow as wonderful as 'a thousand suns'. Glazing and an arched zinc roof that appears to hover above the solid form below punctuate the adjacent ministerial suites building.

The Israeli Foreign Ministry

Sean Stanwick describes how the Canadian firm of Diamond and Schmitt Architects came to produce in the Israeli Foreign Ministry in Jerusalem a building that could be at the same time open and closed, practical and jewel-like.

That architects are called upon to resolve the dichotomy between aesthetics and function is a mandate that is clearly part of the lexicon of architectural design. Yet it is through the resolution of these often divergent concepts that the elegance of architecture is born. This was the task at hand for the Toronto firm of Diamond and Schmitt Architects with the Israeli firm Kolker Kolker Epstein when designing the new Israeli Foreign Ministry – a structure that was to be at once contextually pleasing and inviting, yet also insular and rigorously protected in a highly volatile region.

The project was originally won through an international competition in 1996. Located in the Kiryat Ben-Gurion – a new precinct of government buildings – the $70 million, 419,000-square-foot ministry is one of a sequence of structures that works to create a continuous urban edge along the ceremonial National Boulevard, a ring road that defines the National Precinct within. While given a prominent urban location, not all buildings are afforded the same level of symbolic importance. Again, the conflict arises: how must a building sympathetically reference its context while at the same time expressing its own identity? The solution plays upon this conflict and is a theme that will permeate the entire structure.

Architecturally, the designers responded to these issues with a layered geometric configuration of the site and its four distinct structures set within. Upon arrival, visitors enter the complex via a sunken, oval ceremonial arrival court. Access is provided via a transparent glass checkpoint that forms a controlled aperture to the space. The glass-and-steel cube imparts a sense of welcome and, rather than relying on typical fortified concrete walls, perimeter security is achieved discreetly through the richly landscaped edges of the sunken court.

The ministerial suite, the first building encountered by visiting diplomats, is positioned in alignment with its neighbours along the National Boulevard and works to reinforce the urban edge. This building houses conference rooms, press and meeting rooms, and offices for the deputy minister, the minister and the director-general. Punctuated by an emphatic entrance and a transparent canopy, the upper portion is heavily glazed and topped by an arched zinc roof that appears to hover above the solid form below. Another large, rectangular bar-shaped building situated on the opposite western edge contains administrative offices, a consular department, library and diplomatic school. Although a slab structure by form, a series of five-storey repetitive pavilions with gardens between reduces the scale and massing of the facade and creates a stronger relationship with the street. Linear pergolas on the upper floors of both buildings further help to shade light and soften their hard linear quality.

Sandwiched between these two rectilinear structures is the contrasting elliptical ballroom. Deep apertures designed to emphasise the apparent solidity of the form puncture the sloping stone-clad walls. Half sunken into the ground, the roof is actually more landscape than building; the parapet is a planting trench while a grove of orange trees in oversized pots shades the ballroom below.

Aesthetically, the contextual resolution of these three forms is achieved through the use of Ramon yellow limestone, quarried from the Negev desert. A municipal regulation mandates that all new buildings in the area use Jerusalem stone and, as such, the architects accept it as a key component in communicating the

The simple cubed form of the hall actually belies its complexity of assembly and function. Forming a structural skeleton, 12 tapered concrete columns with calliper-shaped capitals support a glazed roof shaded by a horizontal suspended, perforated aluminium parasol. Attached to this structural assembly are the onyx panels. Only 3 centimetres thick by 38 centimetres high by 60 centimetres long, the panels are suspended on aluminium spring clips. In the event of an explosion, the panels recede inwards on the springs and then recoil outwards, diffusing the force of the blast. To allay the concerns of the hyper security-conscious Israeli government, a full-scale mock-up was constructed. Says Diamond: 'The initial test failed miserably, but the second blast test was a success.' Meeting the strict criteria for security and aesthetics, the innovative facade won an Innovation Award from the Royal Architectural Institute of Canada and is now considered the safest building in the region.

And while it was understood that the ceremonial functions of visiting delegates are granted the highest priority and at times must take precedence over daily operations, the ministry also insisted that in the spirit of democracy the separation of entrances for VIPs and members of staff was wholly unacceptable. 'The primary concern was that the hall should at once be secure but in a manner that would reflect the democratic nature of the state,' says Diamond.

Once again, the designers have imparted upon the architecture a multiplicity of responsibilities and take seriously the position of welcome and accountability. While staff and visiting delegates enter at different entrances on separate levels, they nevertheless both enter through the reception hall. Encircling the hall is a mezzanine with sandblasted glass floors and a teak lattice screen to provide shielded passage without disturbing the formal ceremonies below. Adding yet another layer, the teak screen works with the onyx panels as a sun shield, and as a debris shield in the event of a blast.

In 1967, Naomi Shemer wrote, in what would eventually be regarded as the national song: 'Jerusalem all of gold, Jerusalem bronze and light ... A thousand suns will glow.' With a simple palette of stone and light, the architects have drawn from these words to provide a building that at once democratically makes available its soul while at the same time refusing to yield to prescriptive conventions. And is that not, after all, the spirit of this land? ⵀ+

architectural vernacular of the region. However, instead of using traditional hand-cut pieces, the stone was mechanically cut and applied as tiles to the concrete substructure. Thus, by treating a conventional material with unconventional means, the stone no longer serves as load-bearing and now becomes a delicate appliqué. Through horizontal banding and a range of finishes, from tooled to polished, a traditional material now inherits a Modernist sensibility and, says Jack Diamond, the architect of the project, 'has variety with unity ... and achieves a sophisticated rustication'.

The fourth and final structure in the complex is the reception hall. Probably the most salient reconciliation of the conflict between aesthetics and function, the hall is clearly the jewel in the ministry's crown. While the base is fully glazed to allow maximum light penetration during the day, the top is wrapped in a translucent veil of semiprecious Chinese onyx – a move akin to Bunshaft's Beinecke Rare Book and Manuscript Library at Yale University. The 30-millimetre-thick onyx walls actually perform a double duty by bearing a remarkable similarity to the Ramon stone by day, but emanate a warm amber glow at night. Inside, light penetrates the onyx to flood the space with softly coloured yellow light, enriched by the random iridescence of the veins deep within the stone.

Based in Toronto, Sean Stanwick is a regular contributor to ⵀ who has a particular interest in urban design and the themed spectacular. He has contributed to *Sustaining Architecture in the Anti-Machine Age* (Wiley-Academy) and is currently writing *Wine By Design* and *Reviving the Industrial Aesthetic* (also for Wiley). He is an instructor with the Royal Architectural Institute of Canada and is currently a design architect with Farrow Partnership Architects.

Cyber_Reader
Critical Writings for the Digital Era

Edited by Neil Spiller

Phaidon (London and New York), 2002;
ISBN: 0714840718, 320 pages, £24.95.

Understanding Systems:
Conversations on Epistemology and Ethics

Heinz von Foerster and Bernhard Poerksen

Carl Auer Systeme (Heidelberg), 2002; ; ISBN 0306467526; $64.95

The idea that Cybernetics might be of interest to architects is not new. Indeed, in one of the texts Neil Spiller has selected for his "Cyber_Reader," one of the truly great cyberneticians, Gordon Pask, argued for "The Architectural Relevance of Cybernetics," in a special issue of *Architectural Design* (1969) edited by Royston Landau. Spiller himself, in his fascinating introduction, makes the point that Cedric Price designed the first cybernetic building when he developed his "Generator" project (DDDD). John Frazer, whose book *An Evolutionary Architecture* is also excerpted, developed the computing for Price's project. An argument might be made, however, that the Fun Palace, rather than Generator, was the first cybernetic building: and that project was developed by Price and Pask working together with Joan Littlewood. However that may be, Pask ended his life working with Frazer's Unit at the AA, thus completing a circle of relevance.

I don't wish to labour the point. Many have come to believe that Cybernetics and Architecture bear a close affinity, including me, who studied both! I just want to justify writing about cybernetics and cybernetic issues in an architecture magazine.

Even wearing my cybernetician's hat I find Spiller's book *Cyber_Reader* fascinating. It consists of selections from many key texts that take ideas from cybernetics and related areas and develop them towards notions of machine/human interaction that may find their most extreme form in William Gibson's "CyberSpace"– a notion Spiller charmingly and enlighteningly describes as having started as "a vacant word – a word with no real meaning." Indeed, Spiller's commentary is one of the most interesting aspects of this book, whether (as in this case) in the introduction, or in the short texts that set each selection in context.

Spiller's selection is quite wonderful. His book is remarkable: for the individual items in it, and for their articulated collection together. There are texts in Cyber_Reader I didn't know about, and others I have long wanted to read. There are, too, of course some I'd have liked to include that Spiller didn't; for instance, Heinz von Foerster's paper "On Constructing a Reality."

Von Foerster's book is, perhaps, not so easy to write about in an Architectural magazine as Spiller's book, not because Spiller's is simpler, but because it's more obviously directed towards what architects might consider as their interests, and because the names he mentions are generally familiar.

However, von Foerster's book "Understanding Systems" is, if anything, even more remarkable. It takes the form of the edited and assemble outcome of a series of interviews carried out by the German science journalist, Bernhard Poerksen. Von Foerster's name is probably not well known to readers of ⌂, but his insights have turned cybernetics around in the course of the last 30 years, and Pask, for one, held him in the highest regard, considering him as his mentor. Von Foerster was an extraordinarily cultivated man coming from the most distinguished Austrian family—the family that built the Vienna Ring, whose frequent house guest was architect-philosopher Ludwig Wittgenstein, and who sponsored the alternative 12 tone composer, JM Hauer – and this shows through in the book.

Understanding Systems is a summary of von Foerster's thinking over the course of a long life-time (he died in October 2002). Given von Foerster's background, it is of course, widely read and deeply literate. But so are many accounts. What distinguished von Foerster as a cybernetician was that, towards the end of his "official" academic life he instituted a change in how we understand the systems we examine and interact with. If Spiller's book talks about a new relationship between the imagination and the action, and the physical and the virtual, it is von Foerster around whom developed the conceptual shift that allowed these new dyads to be posited and explored. Von Foerster's switch was to ask how any system could be observed without there being an obeserver to do the observing. He therefore posited a "second order" cybernetics, not about observed systems, but about the observing systems that might observe the observed systems.

This was an astonishingly exciting insight. I remember hearing him talk about it the first time we met, when he was formulating this position and when I was a student at the beginning of my cybernetic studies. The moment you take this step towards the observing rather than the observed, new worlds unfold, and, with them, the sorts of new possibilities we enjoy with Spiller.

These worlds feel very similar to design. For instance, both involve circular arguments/activities in which it becomes apparent that what we know depends on how we choose to look at it, the questions we ask, and the sense we make. In this sense, the many of the insights that derive from second order cybernetics fit very comfortably with design, Of course, many don't: the tendency towards a constructivist position seems contrary to the worlds of physics, legality, and social benefit that architects often try to work within.

Here's where Spiller's book helps complete the circle, for it shows us a whole world that is not and can never be subject to these conventions, but which await the imaginative contribution and the creative acts and interventions of architects who have been, after all, virtual reality engineers for at least 5000 years.

These are two wonderful, fabulous books. One, assembled by a figure well known to readers of $\mathcal{D}$, is full of the most marvelllous texts, texts that bring us both the history and the culture that leads towards today's world of cybernetic insights and comuptational magic within which some architects will be drawn to work. The other, by a genius perhaps unknown in architectural circles (although Lebbeus Woods did illustrate some of his papers), shows how those insights have been forged, and explores the meaning of they can have for how we understand the worlds we make, how we can act, the ethics of how we should act, and who we are.

This year I shall give my students Spiller's book. But last year, and perhaps rather surprisingly, I gave my students von Foerster's book. Every one of them found magic in it, insight, profundity. I met von Foerster last just before he died, and put it to him that his life had been spent exploring wonder. He agreed. What better course is there for any of us?

Reviewed by Ranulph Glanville

London Caffs

Written by Edwin Heathcote
Photography by Sue Barr

As the last vestiges of London's working class culture are being squeezed out by the corporate chains one almost sacred set of spaces survives. The doors into London's caffs reveal a fading, formica and tile-covered world of cheap, basic food, thumbed tabloids, classless bonhomie and a rooted, genuinely local culture. The interiors of these caffs combine a cheery mid-century modernism with the pathos and existential angst of a dying phenomenon. Full, they can be the buzzing heart of a district, heaving, steaming rooms in which all types and classes sit intimately up against one another, empty they can embody a Beckett world of isolation and forlorn anticipation of the encroaching trample of the corporate stranglehold on the city's high streets. The common and instantly recognisable language of interior features embraces the spluttering frothy coffee machines, utility furniture, mosaic tiles, extraordinarily detailed, handwritten menus, glazed sandwich cases and Italian landscapes and boxing posters; an archetypal vocabulary which seems to haunt the city's sub-conscious and crop up in unexpected corners like a welcome and comforting hit of urban déjà vu.

This book selects some of the finest and most representative of this tenacious and indispensable genre and documents them while they continue to thrive or before they finally succumb to decline. It is part gazetteer, part document and part (visual and literal) essay. A homage to one of the city quintessential set of interior spaces.

Edwin Heathcote, London Caffs, ISBN 0470094389, £9.99 PB, Wiley-Academy, August 2004
You can order your copy directly through John Wiley & Sons now using any of the following methods: by phone: +44 1243 843294; by fax: +44 1243 843296; by email: cs-books@wiley.co.uk.
Or you can order it online at www.wileyeurope.com/go/londoncaffs.

Subscribe Now

As an influential and prestigious architectural publication, *Architectural Design* has an almost unrivalled reputation worldwide. Published bimonthly, it successfully combines the currency and topicality of a newsstand journal with the editorial rigour and design qualities of a book. Consistently at the forefront of cultural thought and design since the 1960s, it has time and again proved provocative and inspirational – inspiring theoretical, creative and technological advances. Prominent in the 1980s for the part it played in Postmodernism and then in Deconstruction, △ has recently taken a pioneering role in the technological revolution of the 1990s. With groundbreaking titles dealing with cyberspace and hypersurface architecture, it has pursued the conceptual and critical implications of high-end computer software and virtual realities. △

⚖ Architectural Design

SUBSCRIPTION RATES 2004
Institutional Rate: UK £160
Personal Rate: UK £99
Discount Student* Rate: UK £70
OUTSIDE UK
Institutional Rate: US $240
Personal Rate: US $150
Student* Rate: US $105

*Proof of studentship will be required when placing an order. Prices reflect rates for a 2002 subscription and are subject to change without notice.

TO SUBSCRIBE
Phone your credit card order:
+44 (0)1243 843 828

Fax your credit card order to:
+44 (0)1243 770 432

Email your credit card order to:
cs-journals@wiley.co.uk

Post your credit card or cheque order to:
John Wiley & Sons Ltd.
Journals Administration Department
1 Oldlands Way
Bognor Regis
West Sussex PO22 9SA
UK

Please include your postal delivery address with your order.

All △ volumes are available individually. To place an order please write to:
John Wiley & Sons Ltd
Customer Services
1 Oldlands Way
Bognor Regis
West Sussex PO22 9SA

Please quote the ISBN number of the issue(s) you are ordering.

△ is available to purchase on both a subscription basis and as individual volumes

---

○ I wish to subscribe to △ *Architectural Design* at the **Institutional rate of £160**.

○ I wish to subscribe to △ *Architectural Design* at the **Personal rate of £99**.

○ I wish to subscribe to △ *Architectural Design* at the **Student rate of £70**.

○ △ *Architectural Design* is available to individuals on either a calendar year or rolling annual basis; Institutional subscriptions are only available on a calendar year basis. Tick this box if you would like your Personal or Student subscription on a rolling annual basis.

○ Payment enclosed by Cheque/Money order/Drafts.

Value/Currency £/US$ [   ]

○ Please charge £/US$ [   ] to my credit card.
Account number:

[ ][ ][ ][ ][ ][ ][ ][ ][ ][ ][ ][ ][ ][ ][ ][ ]

Expiry date:

[ ][ ][ ][ ][ ]

Card: Visa/Amex/Mastercard/Eurocard *(delete as applicable)*

Cardholder's signature [   ]

Cardholder's name [   ]

Address [   ]

[   ]

[   ] Post/Zip Code [   ]

Recipient's name [   ]

Address [   ]

[   ]

[   ] Post/Zip Code [   ]

I would like to buy the following issues at £22.50 each:

○ △ 170 *The Challenge of Suburbia*, Ilka + Andreas Ruby
○ △ 169 *Emergence*, Michael Hensel, Achim Menges + Michael Weinstock
○ △ 168 *Extreme Sites*, Deborah Gans + Claire Weisz
○ △ 167 *Property Development*, David Sokol
○ △ 166 *Club Culture*, Eleanor Curtis
○ △ 165 *Urban Flashes Asia*, Nicholas Boyarsky + Peter Lang
○ △ 164 *Home Front: New Developments in Housing*, Lucy Bullivant
○ △ 163 *Art + Architecture*, Ivan Margolius
○ △ 162 *Surface Consciousness*, Mark Taylor
○ △ 161 *Off the Radar*, Brian Carter + Annette LeCuyer
○ △ 160 *Food + Architecture*, Karen A Franck
○ △ 159 *Versioning in Architecture*, SHoP
○ △ 158 *Furniture + Architecture*, Edwin Heathcote
○ △ 157 *Reflexive Architecture*, Neil Spiller
○ △ 156 *Poetics in Architecture*, Leon van Schaik
○ △ 155 *Contemporary Techniques in Architecture*, Ali Rahim
○ △ 154 *Fame and Architecture*, J. Chance and T. Schmiedeknecht
○ △ 153 *Looking Back in Envy*, Jan Kaplicky
○ △ 152 *Green Architecture*, Brian Edwards
○ △ 151 *New Babylonians*, Iain Borden + Sandy McCreery
○ △ 150 *Architecture + Animation*, Bob Fear
○ △ 149 *Young Blood*, Neil Spiller
○ △ 148 *Fashion and Architecture*, Martin Pawley
○ △ 147 *The Tragic in Architecture*, Richard Patterson
○ △ 146 *The Transformable House*, Jonathan Bell and Sally Godwin
○ △ 145 *Contemporary Processes in Architecture*, Ali Rahim

LIGHT RAIL REVIEW 2

CONTENTS

Published by Platform 5 Publishing Ltd. and the Light Rail Transit Association.

Edited by Michael Taplin and Peter Fox.

© Light Rail Transit Association, Albany House, Petty France, London SW1H 9EA and Platform 5 Publishing Ltd., Lydgate House, Lydgate Lane, Sheffield S10 5FH. No part of this publication may be reproduced or transmitted in any form or by any means electronic, mechanical, photocopying, recording or otherwise, without the prior permission of the publisher.

ISBN 1 872524 23 0

Printed by BDC Printing Services Limited, Slack Lane, Derby

Further copies of this publication may be obtained from Platform 5 Publishing Ltd. or the Light Rail Transit Association at the above addresses, price £5.95. Please add 10% (UK) 20% (overseas) to cover postage and packing.

FOREWORD

This second edition of Light Rail Review has been delayed from the originally intended publication date of November 1990 to early 1991, in order to fully cover the South Yorkshire Supertram scheme, which was not given the go-ahead by the Government until 12th December 1990. As a citizen of Sheffield, it gives me great pleasure that Britain's first modern tramway will run in our city, and I look forward to work commencing later this year.

Hopefully, the Midland Metro will be approved this year, but it is too early yet to say whether the change of government will produce any major change in transport policy. The public transport minister, Roger Freeman, declared himself a "great believer in light rail" at the Sheffield press conference. Let us hope that this belief is translated into future action. In particular, let us hope that in future, user-benefits, as well as non-user benefits are taken into account when assessing applications for section 56 funding. To do so would greatly increase the number of schemes which would actually be built, and would remove the need for premium pricing policy. *Peter Fox*

LIGHT RAIL REVIEW 3

will be published in November 1991. Features will include Amsterdam, Birmingham, Manchester and Zürich. Would any potential advertisers please contact Platform 5 Publishing at the above address.

BRITISH CITIES NEED THE LIGHT RAIL EFFECT

As the Department of Transport starts work on a £16 billion programme for national roads, Michael Taplin of the Light Rail Transit Association wonders where all the traffic they generate will go when it reaches our towns and cities, and what life will be like there unless similar sums are invested in environmentally-friendly public transport.

Los Angeles smog is no longer a topic for jokes. As California prepares to introduce the toughest environmental programme in the world to reduce motor vehicle emissions, the sprawling city is turning to rail to woo commuters off the freeways and back to public transport. Since July 1990 Los Angeles and Long Beach have been linked by a light rail line, and work is about to start on a second line, which will serve LAX airport.

Los Angeles doubled the width of its motorways 20 years ago, but then Britain always was 10 years behind with the latest fashion. Now we appear determined to prove that traffic growth forecasts come true, and London-style congestion affects all our major towns and cities. Investment in major urban public transport schemes like light rail seems rationed to one start a year if we are lucky; the rest can make do with diesel buses, which will become more and more unattractive as traffic

ation or development, is no flash in the pan. Local politicians at least have realised that there is no way the capacity of the highway network can be expanded in their own cities without destroying the physical and social fabric they seek to preserve. They still baulk at beating the motorist with a big stick, but see the carrot of high-quality public transport as a means of persuading a switch from the private car.

Light rail is flexible, cost-effective, quiet, clean and comfortable, with the image to attract those who would never ride on a bus (even a guided bus). It costs a lot less than conventional rail, and can even attract private finance (if only the government would give its commitment up-front instead of as a last resort), though never on the scale of the unique London Docklands. What it needs is a streamlined Parliamentary procedure to clear the pending log-jam of Bills, and a dedicated source of public funding – there are plenty of examples to choose from in continental Europe and the USA, including sales taxes, fuel taxes, payroll tax, revenue bonds and road pricing.

Politicians of all persuasions have realised they cannot ignore these arguments, and whilst parliamentary procedures are to be revised, a dedicated funding source needs to be identified and promoted.

SIEMENS

Low-floor articulated cars for in-street and light rail operation.

South Yorkshire Supertram
Double-articulated,
8 axle, light rail vehicle.

For further information
Siemens plc
Energy & Automation
Transportation Systems
Sir William Siemens House
Princess Road, Manchester M20 8UR
Tel: 061 446 5105 Fax: 061 446 5102

DUEWAG

Light rail vehicles for Kassell & Geneva.